ABSTRAXION

Exhibition of literary abstracts

Oarabile Maruatona

ABSTRAXION

Copyright © 2017 by Oarabile Maruatona

ISBN 978-0-646-97099-8

I dedicate this book to my mother Esther
Gaothobogwe Ramosamo and my daughter Unathi
Maya Omaru.

Contents

Prologue

Abstraxion is a collection of just over 40 short pieces. The pieces are diverse in topic, presentation and tone but collectively paint a picture that each reader will interpret according to their understanding and feeling. Each piece is preceded by a synoptic narrative summarising the context of the piece.

Every piece of Abstraxion is about expressing, describing, dreaming, imagining, creating or recreating creatively an idea, a plan, a concept, a useful thought. The Abstraxion is about opportunity, that chance that most of us are waiting for. It can happen on any day, everyday is a *Day of Life,* a day to help materialise the opportunity. Everyday and every-time that one has opportunity and access, one must make it count. If one finds whatever it is that is worth expressing, describing, dreaming, imagining; then one must know that the creation and novel recreation is never in vain. Even if it seems like an *Abstract Jabber,* it will be laden with meaning. Even when it is a simple *Mess Around,* it will be mighty impactful. If *Sebakanyana se,* this little moment allows it, then the old theory of *Leverage* will be re-proposed and re-presented in one of the 40 pieces.

Most of the knowledge, facts, thoughts and everything else in the 40 pieces was inspired by someone else through a song, a book, or some other interaction of some sort. Some of my inspirations in writing Abstraxion include the essays of William Hazlitt, Ralph Emerson and Sam Johnson; the writings of Sun Tzu, Evelin Sullivan and Martin Heidegger; the

i

philosophy of Lao Tzu and the I Ching, the songs of Robert Marley, the stubborn and brilliant unorthodoxy of Fela Kuti, the economics of Adam Smith, the poetry of Hip Hop, the struggles of Nelson Mandela, the Science of Louis Pasteur and the paintings of Goya. I thank these and others whose ideas are somehow adapted into my writings, I hope my book reflects your collective inspiration. Because of you, Abstraxion is not a book about any one thing in particular but envelops a range of perspectives on a range of ideas, thoughts, confusions and concepts.

The story of 40 pieces is for anyone who takes time to read it. For mothers, daughters, sisters and all women, one of the 40 pieces describes the condition of a certain Mokhadi, a woman down on her luck but fighting for her children. The piece of *Woman* details the breakthrough of the daughter of Marble and the ordeal of Nkazi, another woman trying to make thin ends meet. The story of 40 pieces is the story of love. In one of the stories, the storyteller proclaims that *If I got* a life with you, a life so accomplished and fulfilled, then I would consider myself lucky and successful; because you *meine Likle*, are worth a song even if this song is out of tune and *Untitled*.

For those who pray or refer to some supreme being, the story of 40 pieces is my prayer. Dear Yahweh, here is my prayer, hear my SOS. May the 40 texts instruct us to accept one another despite our diversity. May Allah inspire a constructive perception of the *Afro-graphics* and *Cause of Effect*. Insha'Allah the reader connects and identifies with *The man, the good man*; understands the plight of *The Ex-pression* and gets the con of *Commercial*. May the ten gurus guide Miss Digital and all other disadvantaged and minorities as they fight for respect, recognition and reinstatement as equals. Namaste to the Buddha for the inspired moments. It is in such moments that my *Personal PhD* was conceived. It is the same moments that saw *Shorthands* invented, *Personal truths* abstracted and *Wondrous Wanders* traversed. As I acknowledge the murtis, I ask that all my wishes be heard by Shiva. I appeal to Ganesha as I present perspectives on *The squeezed middle,* as I offer a thought on *the Currency of value and virtue* and as I describe the concept of *Notion Development.* Even as I blindly compose poems on *Dried Yarrows,* as I try to capture the persistence of *Recursion* and predict *Che tempo che fa*; I hope the wisdom of Athena permeates my words. I hope the *badimo* nod as I sketch and paint with letters the landscapes of old Egyptian dynasties, deep in the quarters of *Khun Anup*; as I make vivid and liven the journey of *Transitory.*

Abstraxion is abbreviation for Abstract-Exhibition, it is an exhibition of literary abstracts. Some of the 40 exhibited abstracts are spontaneous like *Heat of the Moment,* and grateful like *Nurturing the Dream;* some abstracts are outrageous like falsely accusing another for *farksake.* Although others are selfish, like how I would feel when I die in *Bye World;* others are vigorous *like Upping Ante,* and some are pushy like *Catchyoucatchingacold.* Each of the 40 pieces is a *Recollection* of some thought; it may be a conspiracy on the *Con of Man* or *about the Con-Pression Treatise.* It may be the historical legend of the *Mystique of Umaru*; a philosophical thought on the *Teachings of Con Fuseus* or an opinion on the *Philosophy of Self-preservation,* it is still just a recollection. In some parts, it is just a letter to the *African Scholar* and everyone who cares to be concerned that we, are *Getting new names.* Even if we temporarily get referred to as *Khukhi,* we know we are it.

I wrote Abstraxion to be a book to be read, passed onto a friend, read again, talked about, passed onto another friend and talked about with another friend. But ultimately, I will feel accomplished if just one other person reads it and gets it. This will be enough; and for me *Nuff is Enuff.* If the Abstraxion gets widely read, then I might as well say *Bye World,* do not forget that the power belongs *To You Reader*; you are the biggest piece in the story of 40 pieces. And so to you reader goes the greatest thanks.

1. Notion Development

Notion Development abstracts the thought process behind the writing of the pieces of the book of Abstraxion. *Notion Development* is about the creation of the pieces, the exhibited abstracts. The piece describes the abstraction of perspectives and viewpoints meticulously expressed in each of the other pieces of the book. Each piece is an attempt to present just one of the many ideas, thoughts, angles and perceptions available to every concept. In some pieces, the writer's bias is more obvious than in other pieces. Similarly, some pieces have obfuscated messages and themes, whereas other pieces' messages are plainly presented. In every piece, the reader must engage to follow the train of thought. *Notion Development* describes the scene for this train; a journey to a place where destination is self-determined. This way, the self is the securer of own destiny. *Notion Development* is a template to the pieces of Abstraxion; it is the method to the madness of abstracting the terms of a plot and the moral of the story.

Notion development

Follow the train

Once the setting is secured, the rest follows. The project starts in earnest. The flow resumes, the train rolls. But who secures the setting? How is the setting set and what is the setting anyway? The following is only a perspective of the explanation.

What is the setting?

The setting is the big picture. The setting is the whole thing. The setting is where a bird wants to fly, where the train is headed. The setting is where it all starts, where it ends too. In this context the two, the beginning and end are in concert for a noble undertaking. The usually conventional inconsistency of harmonising known opposites does not apply to this setting since it supports and enhances the noble cause of notion development. Notion development if executed successfully is the development of a people, a fact at a time, a truth at a time, a tiny inspiration at a time. Such is its nobility that it enriches the fellow man. And so, the start and the end do coexist in this sense. Together, these are the coaches of the same train being pulled one after the other in the same direction by some powerful energy. When it is time, even when all may not be aboard, force motion engages, a notion takes off, development springs.

The setting is not illusive; it may be not be easier to capture like a painting does a scenery; it may be a bit sophisticated; its philosophy may be oriented to the teachings of Con Fuseus, unknown and untrusted; its rhythm may be a bit slow but the setting is not illusive. It may be trickier to abstract, unlike the way a radar screen illustrates a weather pattern. It may be some metric deeper or perhaps a horse stronger or any unit superior, but it is not unattainable. The setting is not unconquerable. For any worthy undertaking by any worthy undertaker, all that can be overcome will be overcome and the train takes off. This is the evolution of the notion.

How is the setting set?

The setting is set such that the train is long enough, it is essential to accommodate all willing to take the voyage. No *journeywoman* nor *travellingman* is left behind, not on this journey. The setting is set in a peculiar manner, arranged in a particular way. The setting is amusing; the setting is inspirational; the setting is brave; the setting is hopeful. Although confident, the setting is prejudice free. Despite its imperfection, the setting is real. And so forth the setting of the setting goes. The idea is to identify the train, any train of thought, to get on-board and be consumed by the thought so that a notion can be developed, so that a people can be advanced. If this is done then the realisation that the setting is not as complex as first imagined establishes. It may not even be as mentally troublesome as initially perceived. This is the way the setting is set. Keep up.

The way the setting is set is not fixed. A number of variables determine the setting of the time. Different permutations of the variables produce, as can be imagined, different settings. *Excusez la sous-estimation* if the logic of the previous proposition is too obvious. No pun is ever intended with the seemingly cryptic abstractions such as the proposition on the proportionality of permutations to settings. If the relevance is found, the seeming *cryptiques* are just simple words *peculiarly* arranged such that they

3

express the goodness of the good man, the eloquenece of *Khun Anup*, the ideas of the con and maybe, the philosophy of *Con Fuseus*. The abstractions are the stories, the truths and facts of life. Without the abstractions there is no Abstraxion, so the abstracts are the frame, the proverbial setting. Different variables determine what each abstract is about, including the reader's interpretation. Any arbitrary combination of these variables produces a random arrangement. For this reason, the setting can never really be pre-known unless premeditated in some way and carried out flawlessly, with each respondent behaving as planned. In any other context, the setting is not fixed, it is constantly variable and dynamic. This is the fluidity of the notion.

Who secures the setting?

The securer of the setting is he who cannot be named and she who will not be named. She has no gender, his sex is irrelevant, notwithstanding relevant contexts. The securer has to remain anonymous for security reasons. The securer is everywhere. He is anybody, except when he has to be somebody. He is critical like the engine to a train. For security reasons, the securer is universal. She is common, except when quality demands otherwise. She is pivotal like fuel to combustion. When the securer secures, no matter how random the variables, the notion under development is bound to advance a mind, any mind that is open to the ideas of the notion.

The securer is the self. All else would not be possible if it were any other way. As brief as it may have seemed for those who get lost in the thought, the train of thought must terminate at some point, must arrive at some destination. Everyone who gets it has made it.

When a self-determined destination is reached, nothing must dampen the feeling of conquer. As long as what was set to be done was done, this is an accomplishment. As long as a notion was developed, an idea is in existence and a mind is advanced.

2. Personal PhD: A concept

When the first pieces of Abstraxion were written, it was a labour of love. But it is their peculiar style, consistence and harmony of thought that turned the pieces into a personal doctorate. In this PhD, the philosophy is slightly different if not dodgier than that of a professional and academic PhD. However, the meticulousness and depth of the text of the personal PhD is somewhat equal if not deeper and a little more elegant than that in formal PhDs. Also, the passion of the personal PhD is less suppressed than in a formal academic PhD. The seeming crookedness of the philosophy of the personal PhD does not make it any easier to compile. The text of personal dissertation has a little more sophistication to it than most works submitted in pursuit of a formal qualification. Although personal, it is capable of undergoing and withstanding the same scrutiny that professional exegeses go through. The *Personal PhD* is a train of thought I had been gradually compiling soon after the first year of my formal doctorate studies. The personal PhD promotes the ideal of doing one's best for self, the ideal that for some things, only one's best will suffice.

"I don't understand it, I don't know, I think you are the only one that understands it" –Likle (commenting on this piece)

6

Concept of Personal PhD

When initially conceived, the concept of a personal PhD was bereft of intimate detail, devoid of obvious logic but had a grand objective; to inform, inspire, advance as much as the best doctoral dissertation. The following is the abstract to this concept. Many times, different persons will look at the same thing but will not perceive the same thing. Conscious to alternative perceptions, the personal PhD is a template, customizable to different trains of thought, different mentalities and different attitudes. More important than its *templative* objective is its *personalism*, the principle that *each is to their own*. Despite this deep personalism, the personal PhD must withstand very high standards of contextual scrutiny. If it does, it should and will edify like exegeses, abstractly expressing comprehensions of hypothesised propositions. For some, this personal PhD could also be about determination. The determination to maintain long spells of synergy with oneself, the determination to maintain a steady versatility, adapting readily to changing energies. Any product of labour comprising these sub-elements is worthy of the standards with which best works of art and science are held. When completed, the personal PhD will have the tangible worth of the works of Van Gogh and Mozart; it will possess the aura of the creations of Goya and Beethoven, it will intrigue like the science of Copernicus and Galilei. *Eppur si muove* too, it will move like the mathematics of Calculus. Such are standards for any work fitting the personal PhD, it will have the unique craft of self. It will be original and unique. These qualities will be felt through the work and will radiate from the work. It will challenge fellowman, prompt fellowman, engage and captivate

7

the fellowman. Yet, it is known that some supposedly inspired works do not always appear so to the ordinary taste. This supposedly puts both the creator of the work and the detractor on cautious ground, where both must care to think twice before claiming inspired creativity for the former and passing judgment for the latter. Both must be informed that *apparency* to naked eye is not ingredient to all existence. Some exist but can't be seen. Both must remind their forgetful selves that it may not be felt, smelt or touched, but it may still exist. Both must be cautious to not be too stubborn to assume or question supreme inspirations. Because it is supremely inspired, the personal PhD will either be superior or equal to the level of academic output that qualifies scholars to doctors of philosophy.

In our gladly modern and sadly *consumerist* societies, frequent a times one finds themselves having to trade some passion for profit. This has become the fabric of earning legal tender for most in the economic world. In some cases, some have had to sell *they* souls though most deny it and few are unaware of it. Most of these prefer to cash passion at a capital profit. This is no uncommon occurrence in many a *wall streets*. For some, it is noble to give a little for each half a little received, whereas for some, nobility is earning a little more for each little *invested at interest*. For some still, noble is when one lives off one's passion; yet for others it is corrupt to abuse and exploit passion. For the personal PhD, it is not noble to exploit passion. Instead, nobility is understanding that the more passion one has access to, the more the strength one needs to contain and maintain it without exploit and abuse. Greed; unfortunate that it is cited in the personal PhD but has to, as a cautionary note to those who entertain the thought of abusing passion. Of the said damned word it was defined as the craving to exploit and peddle passion. Those who do it are misguidedly in the trade for some gain but never get content from what they be *greeding* for, no matter how massive a passion they exploit and peddle.

3. Untitled

Some pieces of Abstraxion are happier than others; others are more intense than others. *Untitled* is one of the bitter and sour pieces of Abstraxion. The piece narrates the acrimonious thought of a partner in a 'love' relationship. The discordant abstract of the partner's frustration is untitled, for fear of making an already harsh piece more abrasive. Even in a cat and mouse relationship, it is important to acquire the ability to rise over emotions. Unmanaged emotions have a reputation of taking advantage of the vulnerable.

Untitled

"I don't get you. I don't get this, this situation we find ourselves in. Are you the one that got away? Are you the one we kept catting and mousing about but never got on top of? I certainly don't know but if I were to guess, I would say I don't think so," said the cat in *frustration to the mouse.*

You are my little paradise. You are my shangri-la on a *sabach*, my holiday getaway. You are my zone and space when the coordinates are just right. You are my momentary indulgence, my chance at repose. I keep telling you, you are my chosen, selected of many, most favoured of all. *How-unfortunately-ever*, you done changed. At times you get just a little forgetful, you disengage. I would not wish to believe that you just never were, but who could certainly tell. Even if I attempted to decipher you, what if I misunderstood you, misread your motives? For this reason, I think you were never really gotten, though you been to ghetto and met ghosts of those past.

What if you, when we met, you had ulterior motive? Thought you spotted a chance at big game and came out to spoil it, just for bitch sake. If I had anything to do with it, anything at all- I would say probably not. I would readily say of you *-she had good heart*. To assert of your character, I would describe as you *the kind to not hurt a fly*. But, what is this? How about this here mess? What part of the curriculum of life is this psychological hurdle? In my prayers, I keep asking from whom the temptation cometh. I plead to the power that be to let this cup pass. This is no small matter, it is not so mere. This is potentially destructive; may not have destroyed us yet but might as well. This, we cannot take for granted. Ulterior motive or not, we need to get it together. We cannot afford to be the one that got away to each other. While we have our youth, our party just began, the night is young. We just got started.

This, this thing we have was more than a transaction. This was bigger than some lucrative contract. This was supposed to be real, or was it? Was this not the right way? One of several possible routes, was it not? This is what we thought and decided we wanted. This, we chose consciously, did we not? If it be not what we chose, if it be not a conscious choice, then what did we get ourselves into? It has to be what we each bought into given a self-created image of the *flash-forward*. And so if we did invest in what we thought we would eventually master then we can't be that far off. It makes sense, at least it does in all perspectives explored in attempting to unravel this here mystery. If we are headed to our respective flash forwards then this temper contest is but a temporary detour. These fights must be a stopover to our *flash-forward*, a stopover we would both rather forget. For us it is peculiar- this *flash-forward*, as it is to many others. Everyone's flash-forward is customized to their perception, ambition and supportive action. Perception paints a picture, ambition defines it and action supports realisation activities. As in many other interactions and reactions, variables determine specific results. If the picture is well perceived, and ambition is real and action is active enough, then maybe my *flash-forward* is peace and quiet, a place of calm and *chill*. But what could yours be?

Love, there may well be nothing of the sort. It may just as well be a conspiracy, a successful scheme that feeds off emotion, exploiting feelings and abusing passion. If there was no love, if what we know as love existed not then how cruel this world would be. A sorry place where affectionate gestures are no more than transactions, easily exchangeable and bound by contract if need be. In our world of no-love, nothing is worthwhile outside of its cash value, everything has its price, equivalent to some measure of legal tender. If this is truly our world then we are victims of our world. I know this is not the flash-forward we each self-created. I know I am a victim, I believe you are too. I believe that you and I are in the same boat. Don't be alarmed, the world of no-love is only a worst case scenario. In the ideal world, love exists, it is a lover's world. The lover appreciates that even in the ideal world, love cannot be cheap and carries with it a certain value; appreciating love appreciates this value. When this value appreciates, so does some particular significance. This we cannot take for granted either, that even in the ideal world, love is to be embraced, savoured yet paid constant consciousness. Such it deserves and such it commands. Such it is owed, to it, such is due. All these, the lover must appreciate. The amateur at love should not be frowned upon. Generations have struggled to decipher the very core of it. A select few, if any- truly get it and these too, do not get all of it. Some have confessed that luck is the variable that matters most in this setting because it has a lot to do with it. So when it is asked of love, again and again it must be well thought. Thorough ponder is required before suggestions are thrown to the effect of its non-existence. Despite knowing all these, the lover in frustration quietly proclaims that of love, there is nothing of the sort.

And my charge? What was my fault? What was it I did to upset the setting of our love? Turns out you have no charge against me. Against me, no fault was

13

determined, not in definite terms. There was of course the uncertain allegation, a baseless accusation, a fear. The allegation was rebellion, not against supreme powers, nor against world systems. Even for the system, the default status is innocent until proven guilty. My guilt was never ascertained, so don't you dare convict me. You accused me based on uniformed innuendo and doubt. You failed to induce by any logic that if your allegation was true then whatever I am alleged to have done would not have been on false motive. You cannot justify how it was to a bad end that the otherwise just act was transgressed. It could not have been exclusively for selfish indulgence since I was bound by my love for you and was, in that moment incapable of any harm to you. It could not have been intended to hurt you. Since I feel like I am on trial, I would like you to know; that it may have been a selfish act but to the charge you wish to lay on me, I plead not guilty. For lack of associative evidence, I argue that your charges be nullified. I cite lack of clarity in the alleged misdeed. Your misinterpretation of my motive lead you to the misclassification of my inspired deed to what you thought as meditated misdeed.

And the way forward for us? It is still what it was, and what it will always be as it was shown in the *flash-forward*. The *flash-forward* independently perceived by you and I, and jointly aspired to, worked, fought and lived for. The *flash-forward* whose ideal is frequently pledged to in the three short words. So if there is anything you need to comprehend about the way forward, it is that it may not be comprehensive at all times; it may seem hard most times and it may only be guaranteed on some condition. But comprehend this the most; it is worth it anytime. The way forward is that ulterior motive or not, misdeed or not, the pursuit of our *flash-forward* continues. What we each have to do, we do, to enhance our *flash-forward*. What is yours by the way, your *flash-forward*?

"It is a long shot. The interest compounds steadily at a fixed rate, which is credited annually. So you wait and keep waiting. If it fails you give it another chance. And another if it fails again. Dear as it costs initially, your investment accrues to your benefit, slowly cancelling your deficit" –advised the banker to an audience of investors.

4. Sebakanyana se/ this little chance

Being the everyday person means some pursuits take the backburner so that financially generating occupations take precedence. For the same reasons, the writing of Abstraxion had to compete with other activities and occupations of the everyday person. Sometimes the writing got assigned the least priority. However, whenever a little chance presented itself, there was never an ounce of hesitation to put thought to paper. 'Sebakanyana se' is a Tswana phrase meaning -*this little chance.* The piece acknowledges the little chances; that they must be embraced just as one would a great opportunity. The realisation, immediate pursuit and ultimate conquer of the little chance is usually a good indication of how a comparatively bigger opportunity will be handled. *Sebakanyana se* is one of the pieces that were initially handwritten and subsequently typed when the pieces were compiled into a book.

Sebakanyana se (this little chance)

This little chance afforded,
ambitious, creative and visionary forces combining,
rare occasion, rare undertaking.
And so begins the legend of the little chance.
The little chance *some-a-times*,
is the telltale of how one is bound to respond
when big chances abound.
Some have said of the little chance,
that it is a prospect for the unlucky,
to create the luck of the big chance.
A life lived waiting for some lucky break,
is a *life-full* opportunities wasted.
In respect to the small chance,
isn't it best then to dedicate,
some thought to this small chance?
It must be.

This here, right this moment,
is a rare opportunity,
appearing between chaotic commotions.
This opportune moment,
if missed indicates probable chances,
of missing bigger opportunities;
or so goes the moral of small opportunities.
It is in brief moments,
that the magic of all magic happens,
when the *deepwater* creature surfaces to catch a
breath.
One small moment, one giant leap,
one inhale, one dive back into sea.
It is over in no time.
All it took was a little chance.

It is a momentous time,
when the *mannlich* bird of the tropics,
spreads his illusionary wings,
trots briefly for his dame friend.
Studiously he maintains his rhythm.
And if he be lucky, in that lucky moment,
she is baffled but intrigued.
In the same instance,
the two cordially agree to a quick shag.
All in a good little moment.

The little chance is enchanted,
prime time to impose on impossibility.
It is the moments few and far between,
when *any* is absolutely *any*,
when anybody who is anyhow and anywhere,
in appreciation of the little chance,
engages anything accordingly.
It is not unworthy, it can never be wrong,
not if *any is any*.

The biggest tree there ever was,
was apparently once just a seed.
Yet again, the tale of short moments illustrated.
Because unaided, the naked eye has not seen a
seedling grow.
The seedling grows in very brief moments,
too brief for the naked eye.
This is not the mystique. The true wonder is;
that the seedling knows to exploit this moment.
From a tiny seedling, barely emerging from ground,
to a giant structure, a natural landmark.
The seedling takes its chances,
No matter how brief.

So for this little while,
readiness for the small chance,
must be a daring enough conclusion.
To the story of this little moment,
Sebakanyana se.

5. Recollections

Some books are not meant to be read once and stored away. Abstraxion is intended to be a book to read, keep and read again. There is mostly no story to remember, no logic to follow. It is a peculiar collection of facts, thoughts, observations, feelings, opinions, propositions and imaginations. Some of such thoughts are recorded in the *Recollections*. In *Recollections*, the *recollector* shares thoughts on money, growing up, confusion about things, self-imposed exile and more. The day *Recollections* was written was one of them cloudy cool Sunday countryside afternoons. The air was fresh and clean, the quiet hood was even quieter, the mood was mellow. The kind of day where pausing and recollecting is the best thing to do. Herein is a succinct account of some of my recollections; a random recollection of confusions and questions which we all may have on occasion.

Recollections

Back in the day, a thought that used to dominate my other thoughts is the thought of money. *Moneys* for possessions and acquisitions; acquisition of a comfort; proper, humane and inspiring comfort. Maybe not so much luxury for now, but she is welcome if she is within reach. Could I manage her if I had her? Who knows for sure? Despite my confusion, the thought lingered and the questions remained unanswered. And for some reason, my mind is still on the money. Even though some of my confusions have started to get clearer, I still wonder about money, just how much is enough for mine and my kin's comfort.

The other day I was thinking about my plan. The plan was never to overstay in my part-self and part-situation induced exile. The plan was to play some big role in my *qaeda*. The plan was not just to play some consumer and spectator role for I knew that such would be hollow, short-lived and short-thought. Giving back to my people was always in the books, mostly for the noble reason but also for the selfish aspect of it. Giving has always been in my dreams for progress. I stand not for a brand but for an ideal; Not for provocation but for inclusivity in diversity. Despite my failures at my grand plans, I have not lived in self-imposed exile in despair and longing. If anything the exile has been pivotal in my transformation in becoming a better thinker, a better *expressor* and a better person. In this exile, I have moved from strength to strength. This exile has been my refuge and shelter while I get ready to be of use to the people of the *shango*. Although temptation lingers, the relative comfort in exile must not obstruct my perception of my big picture. I may not be home but with every breath I strive to maintain a strong relevance, both in my exile and at my home.

On other days, I just think about the days themselves. The days are different. Each day brings with it a seemingly familiar but subtly unique feeling. There are days I wish I could chance upon a giant wave and ride its crest like a surfer. Wishing is only useful for *wishfulness*, so I also have to have animal instinct. Like a predator, I must instantly transform to stealth mode and get ready to pounce on opportunity if one is about. So when that wave forms, I must be in time to ride it. It is not always smooth sailing, accidents happen often, distractions line the path of the journeyman. In the interest of my survival I cannot give up and accept the situation, I cannot give in to popular belief. Popular belief has dictated direction for the masses for a while. Multitudes have outsourced thinking and blindly consume popular belief with little doubt. This is the popular belief *modernly* dictated by those with the means and capital to broadcast to the masses. Naturally propaganda, it is spun into some fact, some *faux-truth;* the poor masses have no way of telling what is and what is not. The masses with little time and care to discern the constant feed of untruth, consume it with ease.

Some days I cannot help but look back. Looking back, I always think that growing up was fun. It was fun for me because I expended some effort to ensure it was so. Growing up, I have met a few fellow confused who through interactions of sorts with them, taught me a neat trick or two. These I remember fondly. For each recollection I have about each of them, I disperse a smile, I exhale some positivity in their honour. My recollection of them and others who share their knowledge is also a prayer that they get the happiness they ought to have. I pray that when there are no crests in their waves, they have the attitude to get out and find what they can. And for each trick I learnt from them, I hope I get the opportunity to teach it to another.

Most days when I was younger, I could not really be for or against it; this was my take on it. To this day, I still decide to be undecided on it. When I used to think about it, I could not decide if I felt leftist or had right winged tendencies on the matter. I chose to be neither liberal nor conservative on the idea of it. I just wanted the ideal, I wished for perfection. I may have been young then, innocent in some way and naive to some degree. I was a novice at it and had not been in it for long. *Amy* had sung passionately that it was a losing hand. I used to wonder whether she herself heard it from some other song or whether she learnt this from some other lover of hers. I had personally felt it, not that it is a losing hand but that it just is. I momentarily had it before it all got confusing. But I was also most thankful at the time that I had a good head but I also regretted that I used my good head to create a hell of a life for myself. I was also grateful for the good people circumstances had placed around me at different times and stages of my life. Back then I wished that if ever I discover that it is non-existent or that it is a losing hand, then this happens when I am old enough. For that time however, I preferred to momentarily indulge in whatever I had. I did not care to name it, it might have been it. I preferred this over accepting that it did not exist. I preferred the self-delusion over accepting that those who believed in it were holding a losing hand. The more I thought of it, the more I began to imagine that it could not just be an abyss. If it was good enough to *seem* and feel like love, it just could not be nothing. My take on it these days has become more confusing.

Some days I realise that I am still as confused as have ever been. The only thing I appear to learn consistently is that the more I know, the more I realise how much I do not know. It did not excite me but it worried me that I had Einstein thoughts. Like many I had been searching for truth in anything I came across. At some points in my truth seeking journey, I depended on logic for understanding and reasoning. I also tried alternative approaches; liked and used some of them too. I then learnt through some philosophy that in life as in anything else, not all is logical. About death, I knew that no living man had any experience on it. But what holds it all together then? What of this god particle? Apparently the grand equation of it all is a little complex for simple minds but fathomable to those who attempt to rise above the ordinary. To cope with the confusion, some humble ideology encourages accepting what is uncontrollable and changing only what is accepted as controllable. When I got fed up with accepted truths, I used to challenge that impossibility. And, using my illogical mental resources, I deduced and concluded that possibility is immeasurable.

And on other days, I ride the spirit train. I pray for all who have given up. In faith I pray that it eventuates for them; that the moment their unbelief is dispelled eventuates sooner than later. Then they can doubt no-more but can believe more, then they will have the confidence that they too are worth it, the knowledge that with some effort, they can do it. I pray that I never meet anyone with no dreams because all the dreams they had have come true. If such persons exist somewhere, they cannot be as accomplished as it sounds. Apparently the calm we wish for is right in the chaos we live through. Within the illogical is the deepest of logics, apparently. In the spirit of spirituality, this is where I acknowledge the higher powers because even though it may be bliss, ignorance can only sustain to some finite extent.

6. About the Con-Pression Treatise

The Con-Pression treatise is a 16th century exposition on revolution, mental emancipation, war and government. It is singled-out by several authoritative publications on modern economics, philosophy and politics as one of the most influential pieces of literature ever written on the said combination of subjects. Considering when it was first published circa 1500, the significance of this rarely known dissertation is unmistakable. *About the Con-Pression Treatise* summarises some of the most fascinating facts and myths surrounding this timeless masterpiece. This piece provides an excellent overview of the treatise, a worthwhile introduction for those who are not familiar with the Con-Pression treatise. *About the Con-Pression Treatise* collates different facts on the content and context of the writing of the so called treatise of the 16th Century.

About the Con-Pression Treatise

Con-authored

Controversial is how it was described by most and subsequently mostly described. Confusing is what another grouping, bound by a common lack of imagination found it. Some have described its depth as conveniently hiding its incomprehensibility. Still, many others found it to be a hotpot of half-baked philosophies. The *conspiracy of con-pression* also known as the *compression-conspiracy* or Con-Pression treatise, was described by its writer as a treatise whose objective was to concurrently concatenate and connect concept to control; self-control. The writer, hitherto only referred to only as *the Con*, acknowledges that the ideas expressed in the text may seem concealed at initial perusal but that constancy will *unconceal* that before hidden. To date, it is inconclusive if the Con referred to a group of sophisticated scribes and strategists or an individual with the *imaginatory-capacity* of a group of sophisticated scribes and strategists. It is for these and many other reasons that the Con-Pression treatise is usually referred to as the best literary piece of the 16th century.

Coney Contagion

After decades of being constricted to top secret classification and banned for a host of reasons, the treatise gained prominence and widespread acceptance as a compelling and authoritative piece of literature once more in *contura-10-10*, the 20th century, some four centuries after it was first published. Convictive as it was, the ideas of the treatise spread like a volatile contagion. Records of history

27

suggest that the spread of the Coney infection of 1488 was nowhere near as rapid as the dispersion of the ideas of the Con-Pression treatise. The confusion depicted in illustrations of the commotion during the Coney epidemic is compelling. The convincingly gloomy sketches capture the landscape soon after the settlers of *Atlantica* discovered that their staple food, the coney fish was a poisonous species with a slow killing bacterial venom. Once ingested through the fish, the bacteria in the venom would continually infuse organ paralysing enzymes into the bloodstream. The constant organ failure would give rise to an illness which was communicable to anyone within the breath of the infected individual. The consequence was catastrophic. This is the compressed version of the Coney contagion of 1488, and yet just fifty years later certain views of history were starting to compare this contagion to the spread of the readership of the Con-Pression treatise.

Konsapien the conservative

The treatise was originally penned and published under a false name. The entire text comprises three volumes. *Konsapien XIX*, a brutal ruler in the region is believed to have destroyed most copies of the first volume. However, a few more copies remained. It was just before and just after the assassination of *Konsapien* that volumes two and three were respectively published under the name of The Con. Before his uneventful termination, Konsapien had repeatedly tried to use his vast power and wealth but failed to unearth the author of a piece of writing he had grown to fear. He loathed the Con-Pression treatise with all he had; and this was a man who had it all. The Konsapiens had ruled all of the *Congo continents* for centuries between 1440 and 1792. They are unquestionably one of the longest ruling dynasties in the history of government. In disdain to the total control he had on his people, a sophisticated revolt manual was penned and falsely attributed to Konspien XIX to ensure *not-only* wide circulation but also duty of obedience to those who dared question the content of the piece. The last custodian of the Konsapien dynasty was the 19th *kong*, Konsapien XIX. He was a confused conservative obsessed with tradition and routine no matter how inconvenient to common purpose. In his tenure as kong of the Congo, he imposed strict controls on the creation and distribution of free thought and other creative works. This is why many believe the credible conceit that the treatise was an elaborate conspiracy by thinkers of the late 1700s to end the barbaric tenure of *kong* Konsapien XIX. Many *in the know* assert that the treatise was masterfully crafted to exploit the insecurities and predictable aloofness constantly characterised by the 19th *kong*. The assassin who butchered the 19th Konsapien ruler declared soon after the murder, that she murdered *kong* for his lack of simple congeniality. It was for the same reason that the Konsapien's close advisors conspired against him and collectively choreographed his vengeful murder. The assassin had been the Konila, the kong's wife of more than 10 years. Many believe that 10 years is a period it took to pull off the daring murder and the collapse of an enduring dynasty. Konila has since been credited as one of the bravest women of the 16th Century.

Correcting contradiction

Having banned the first volume as a mind contaminant and having described it as absolutely unconducive to any level of intellect, the ruler of the

29

Congo issued a decree to destroy all copies of the Con-Pression treatise. Compelled by the constant show of brutality, the *Congans* were forced to oblige and consequently submitted their copies to be burned at public burning ceremonies. Very few copies were spared, held secretly by their owners, despite knowing that the ultimate price for holding these volumes was capital punishment. Clandestine readings were held in hidden locations. The few who braved the risk of death to attend these readings secretly identified themselves as a *con-munity*, a cohort of the Con-Pression content sympathisers. Many writings on the Konsapien dynasty suggest it was the con-munity who chiefly contributed actionable thought to the *1788 con-mutiny* that resulted in the ultimately fall of the empire. Just before the overthrow, the second volume of the treatise was released. The opening text declared an intention to correct the contradictions of the Konsapien regime and any other authority that dared to control free thought. In the same piece it is asserted that the first and second Con-Pression discourses were authored by the Con, a soul neither related nor consanguineous to the ruling Konsapiens. To the *Congans*, the statement was a confession to the ruled and a confrontation to the rulers who had failed to identify the author of the Con-Pression. The same theme is consistently maintained in subsequent writings of the Con-Pression treatise.

Confabulation protocol

By 1800, some ten years after the collapse of the Konsapien empire in the old Congo, very few copies of the first volume of the Con-Pression treatise remained since most had been destroyed by imperial order. The surviving copies were in the hands of a select few *con-munity* members who had risked death to preserve the ideas of the Con-Pression. When the other two volumes of the Con-Pression were published, it was the few con-munity members who had the complete text and fully understood the ideas of the Con. When the *Convalian* army rose to prominence after the fall of the 19th Konsapien, the Con-Pression was declared a warrior's manifesto. Some extracts of the Con-Pression were read to the conscripts upon their coercion into joining the *Convalian* army. The army initially consisted of a contingent of former soldiers in the previous Konsapien force who had secretly but constantly read and studied the Con-Pression treatise. Convalian warriors were commanded to continually contemplate on the text of the Con-Pression as well as continuously referring to and quoting it in conversations with fellow officers. Since it was a critical command, those found in breach of the *confabulation protocol* were charged with high treason and condemned to death.

Conglomerate of the Congo

The *conal* volume of the Con-Pression treatise was published just after the murder and overthrow of Konsapien XIX. In emphasising unity, its value and strategic importance as a foundation of wealth to the people, the treatise describes the discipline required when factions of separate entities connive towards a common unambiguous bargain. Meticulously, the Con-Pression states the conviction demanded of a *con-munity* member and the qualities that constitute membership in this con-munity. For *con-munity* gatherings, the exposition explains who the convening party should comprise and the authority with which to determine an ideological convergence for an issue of contention. On financial pursuits, the Con-pression cautions *con-munities* against *greeding* in contracts.

31

The treatise advises that it is unconditionally unwise to engage in the commissioning of contemporaneous contracts founded on a permanently consolidated and non-divisible *con-modity*. Other specifications of the treatise on the issue of conniving to a common bargain include the conditions of belonging to the people's congress. The treatise states that the congress will consist of members of consistent integrity and good conduct. Their con-munity duties will range from being constables of the peace, to coordinating plenaries, to convening confidential strategic congregations. They will fairly counsel and adjudicate in con-munity conflicts and deservedly confer awards for acts of heroism, scholastic excellence, and outstanding artistic creation. Those meeting the specified condition and contributing to the execution of any of the stated duties will hold the consecrated office of the people's congress. Conscious of compromise and effective through conjugation of ideas, they will constitute the executive of the chattered conglomerate of the Congo.

7. Dried Yarrow

Abstraxion is about seeing, perceiving, interpreting and expressing. Every piece of Abstraxion expresses alternativism; each piece pays regard to the unique story in each of us, the beauty of everything. One such beauty is expressed in the *Dried Yarrow*. On a table, sits a handcrafted jar. Protruding out of the jar is a green-brown drying yarrow, its slim stem standing firm beyond the mouth of the jar. A few days earlier, the yarrow had been a part of a beautiful bouquet of flowers bought for a loved one. As the days passed the brightest and liveliest rose browned out and lost shine, its sweet smell gone with it. And so followed the ester and others which had also been part of the bouquet. But that was not the case with the yarrow. *Dried Yarrow* is for such as us. Us who ignore our apparent mortality and see the need to fight the good fight.

Dried Yarrow

Once a symbol of beauty,
an object of affection.
Once displayed to reflect,
to reflect love,
a love so ardent.
Now an item to be rid of,
evidence of the past.
Evidence of the effect,
the effect of time.

Exotic of the bunch,
you represented the unique.
You stood with the best,
bright esters and fragrant lilies.
Assembled to make a statement,
composed to impress,
put together to remind and assure.

One by one they wilted.
But you persisted.
You outlasted them all.
Outlived beauty, awe and sweet.
Alien by origin,
you were adaptive at life.
Though you stand dried,
you still stand tall.
Though you stand alone,
You still stand strong.

Outlasted rose and bloom,
out-survived vetch and tulip.
You never asked for much;
a sip of water, a ray of light.

Your vase was makeshift but handcrafted.
Your gifting was selfish but heartfelt.
Once immersed in the water,
you absorbed and flourished.
But over time you got burnt,
your energy, spent and wasted.

Neither outstanding nor dominant,
nor dull nor latent.
Neither rosy nor thorny,
nor and bloomy and pretty.
Subtle you looked, herby you smelled.
Cohabited with a rose,
coexisted in a bunch.
Competed with colour,
battled for longevity.
Survived the short term,
but was only mortal.
Had to happen in the ultimate.
Methodical, you fought the good fight,
tactically, you pursued self-preservation.

Thin branch, slim stem.
Small leaves, petit petals.
Travelled light, packed little calorie.
Lived on the mystical; light and water.
Invested not on the physical,
economic with colour.
Sense provoking scent,
wore it to the end.
Gracefully different,
inspirational through simplicity.

Never looked like much,
ever the underdog.

Either your game is robust,
or your luck abounds.
But there was one other,
with whom you stood no chance.
Time is superior,
has the patience, thrives on endurance.
Time is stronger,
even you had to succumb.

As your stem dries, rest assured,
the meek shall not inherit your vase.
Your not dead,
your leaves just dried,
your colour's just pale,
photosynthesis's blacked out,
botany's bailed,
and your system's failed.
But your not dead.

As your leaves wilt, rest assured,
that your story endures.
Your inspiration will be re-expressed,
Your legend retold.
The legend of the dried yarrow.

8. Philosophy of Self-preservation

'In all philosophies, no philosophy is greater than the philosophy of advancement and enrichment of the self. But even greater is the act of the preservation of self'. These are the words of Con Fuseus, a less known mythical philosopher. The *Philosophy of Self-Preservation* is an attempt to decipher selfishness from a non-selfish perspective. Sufficient effort was spent to ensure that the piece remains as was thought at the time, a pure translation of thought. It is raw, illogical, abstract and dubious. To this piece, one is advised to not be vulnerable to its charms, to be wary of the gentle pulls of the words. The craft and configuration of the words is a smaller part of the greater magic. Instead, the subtle reading between the lines and the decryption of the abstract ramble is what would most probably blow one's mind. So be ye wary.

Philosophy of Self-Preservation

Of Self-preservation it was once said, by a certain darer.

Self-preservation has once or twice been socially cited as one of life's basic and most essential instincts. This *basicness and essentiality* is ambiguous, devoid of definitive specifics, potentially vulnerable to technicality of fact. But these basicness and essentiality are also real. In some circumstances, self-preservation is a basic and most essential life instinct. In most instances, self-preservation is actual. Some are predators, some are prey but irrespective of whether one hunts or gets hunted, the *basicness* and *essentiality* of self-preservation is unquestionable.

In addition to being instinctive, self-preservation underlines an important sense. For the modernist, self-preservation can be taught and learnt, it can be encountered in everyday life, it is in many living-things and lives on many things. On many information avenues, many words have been used to describe self-preservation. It is in the same avenues where too great a false presentation on self-preservation has been distributed, sold, bought and consumed. One ought not to go into further detail than the previous statement on conventional avenues and the propaganda they deal in. The modernist ought to know these.

Henceforth continues the thought of the darer;

If the smallest of creatures are armed with some of the most brutal of accessories to self-preserve, what then of bigger, supposedly stronger creatures? And how about the *neurologically* sophisticated, what of their resolve to self-preserve? And the sexually inferior, how much of this resolve do they have? Is it the male who have it more than the females? Male domination on several human attributes is common. It also not uncommon that in some societies, females call the shots- all sorts. Typical of these sorts of female superiority is the black widow in some arachnid family. She is a widow because she kills and usually eats her husbands and lovers just after she fucks them. She is probably rarely bothered by her cannibalistic tendencies, all her children had been fathered by different males, all of whom she killed and had for dinner, raw too. Another instance where girls run the world is in many insect families. In many of these circles it is all *for queen and colony*. In many of these families, selected males can only mate with only one female, the queen. The rest slave away for queen and colony. If ever *girl- power* was a matter of doubt.

Male or female, dominating or dominated, big and small, all things living have the thing to self-preserve. The industry of insects has inspired several proverbs. *Busy as bees, disciplined as ants*, their self-preservation routines have become philosophies to humans. Insects are proven survivalists, they thrive in many of the harshest conditions. An army of ants dragging a dead, giant cockroach to their underground base in a scorching desert sand is but a typical example. Their command, loyalty and common purpose are not obvious in the patterns of their movements but their urgency is unmistakable, as is their sense of cooperation. They pull together, and pull very well together. This is how much preservation of their selves means to them, and how much a need to

39

maintain this constant prolonging of existence had coerced them into *perpetual strivers*.

Apparently you are what you do; so if what you do is visualise and contextualise, then you are the *visualisor-contextualisor*; one who invests effort to the demands of the cause; the cause of expressing insight; the cause of one's self-preservation. Of this *visualisor-contextualisor*, do not be swayed by her presentation although elaborate, pay attention to her relevance, for therein is the source of her inspiration and the meaning of her self-preservation. So whatever it is you do, whoever it is you are, do not ever be distant to the cause of your self-preservation. If it is exclusively selfish, it is absolutely not right. Make it noble, make it greater than you.

Self-preservation in humans is probably more strategic than in any other living-thing with a need to self-preserve. Compared to all other living-things, humans are neurologically on another level; on another mental level. Humans' sense of learning and calculation is arguably a little more sophisticated than of any other *mammal, amphibius, bird, reptilus* and *insectus*. How successful these animals are in preserving their selves is pivoted on their primal survival accessories, relative strength, relative speed and so relative forth. For the human too, the success of self-preservation has a bit more to do with the very object through which his advantage lies, a sophisticated capacity to learn and calculate. The human uses this capacity to his advantage, usually with the primary objective of survival for some and immortality for others; that I live long and if I should die, then a part of me lives on, and if it should die, a part of it lives on. Self-preservation dictates that all living-things be adaptive to their environments and many do adapt in various ways. The human however, has proven to be a little more adaptive, inventing killing tools to eliminate competition when survival favours the fittest; and turning swords to ploughshares when needs dictate. The human is also a little more resourceful, knows that a man's trash is another's treasure. In many cases, he is a little more spiritual; is in touch with his mind, body and soul. All these to live a little longer, all these to self-preserve.

So humans, blessed with superiority of mind, also find themselves at the mercy of the worst of conditions in animal kingdom- *mental irrelevance.* Once in a while, a human gets lost and gets a bit more confused than the average fellow. Even more confusing is when this irrelevance falls upon a man who seems to have it all, an enviable life. But then given the exclusivity afforded by wealth, many a poor man will never understand the disease of the aristocrat. It is near impossible to emulate his diet, it is not viable to afford his pleasures; one can't begin to imagine what he stuffs in his pipe. These are but a few of the obstacles to establishing cause of effect when the seemingly accomplished harbours suicidal attitudes. Irrespective of his cause, it is not uncommon to hear of the wealthy man's sudden disgust with his seemingly successful endeavour at self-preservation.

The idea of a mind, body and soul is widely accepted yet few understand the significance of an enduring balance between a sound mind, a healthy body and a settled soul to self-preservation. They matter, very much. For the mind, body and soul, nurture is a significant element. Most ideologies advocate for a balance of these threesome; some preach familiarity and harmony with *father, son and spirit*; the holy trilogy often represented by the mind, body and soul in alternative perspectives. Of the three, none is more important than the others and all determine the quality and duration of one's existence. The physicality of the body serves the mind and soul. The mind dictates to the body the specifics of the said service. The soul is the body's connection to everything non-physical and the mind's adapter to all things non-mental. All three harmonise respective functions to self-preserve. The imperfection of this harmony is what each of us is personally and how hard, how deep and how spiritual each of us will go to self-preserve.

And so for humans, as is for everything else living, the pursuit of self-preservation continues everyday. The *duration and quality* of this pursuit fluctuates in different settings, according to conditional variables and effects. It has become apparent to some that the *duration and quality,* although dissimilar, have a curious dependence on one another. A common attitude on the matter of *duration and quality* suggests that those with a better quality, and to an extent those who appreciate and actively nourish their lives, usually yearn for a longer duration. It is for this reason that a desperately sick and bedridden *khulu* cries *Modimo-Nkutswa** at his hour of need, because he is at the receiving end of life's worst quality. For this sick chick, the duration is not relevant because the quality is at its extreme worst. Many more have and would probably choose to terminate duration of existence if the quality of the existence is desperate.

It has been advised that what we ingest is what we excrete, exhale and express. We are cautioned to watch what we ingest, lest we consume toxicity and excrete, exhale and express toxicity. In our *consumes*, we are advised to be modest, and to be never in excess. As much as thought is free, it pays to invest in it. It is wise to watch what one wishes for in case one gets just that. Whereas the pessimist, true to his nature, may conclude cynically that the reason beggars do not ride is because wishes are not horses; the optimist insists that *half empty* or *half full*, it never hurts to wish for better. Anyone is better off a step closer than two away from a desirable state, some favourable quality, some additional contributor to a longer duration. Whereas the notion of *half full* comforts the optimist with the hope that enough is enough, the *half empty* attitude allows the pessimist the courage to accept and live with the little they have. Both perspectives are respectively worthwhile to the pursuits of self-preservation for the pessimist and the optimist.

Self-preservation is peculiar to each and unique to other. The duration and quality that accompany this preservation are relative to the character and attitude of the *self-preservationist*. The preservation of self in as humble an attitude as can be found is never about not wanting to die prematurely but about using every opportunity to be as helpful to others as one can humanly be. In reverence to this ideal, many unwittingly become convicts of righteousness, in their futile effort to traverse the path of faultlessness. And if one seeks a life of quality, keeping well physically, mentally and spiritually is a recommended habit. In other ideologies, seeking the favour of a supreme being is all there is to it; the quality and duration of one's life. In alternative cultures, sacrifices to gods increase one's chance at living longer, no matter how miserable they may be. For such as these, the gods prefer virgin lambs for the sacrifice of absolution. The lamb represents life at its incorrupt state, an illusion of the faultlessness that the sacrificer seeks. For the faultless, the poor lambs who get burnt in the name of sacrifice, apparently their honour is in the next life. Apparently nothing is as honourable as being sacrificed for the gods. So, no matter how humble and selfless one's self-preservation exercise is, it is still a treacherous path. If there is no after life, some acts of kindness may not return on investment. The treacherousness of this path is also the uniqueness, imperfection and mortality of our respective self-preservation acts.

Relative to the supposed vanity of perfection, what good is it to be an anomaly? Does it help to be one of the few best or the mediocre majority? For a given setting, compared to a non-outlier, an anomaly has very slim chances of being detected by a system, any detection system. This is enabled by the anomaly's scarcity relative to the entire set. In some settings, the system may classify the anomaly as a false positive. For the false positive, things can only get better if the current given category is contextually not preferable. For the false negative, this position in the same context is worth preserving because anything else is worse. For any other classification, it is worthwhile not having a false tag. One therefore must self-resolve to never be false; must self-assure constantly that one is being oneself. This, according to some is how one truly self-preserves.

And this darer, identified as Con Fuseus dared that hoper gets and that seeker finds.

*God steal me

44

9. Wondrous wander

The *Wondrous wander* is a celebration of the creation process, an expression of the admiration of creativity. The wondrous wander is a series of undirected wanderings of thought. The piece records some of these wanderings. A wander on perfection notes that the blind pursuit of perfection is a possible deterrent to creativity and creation. The wanderer suggests that instead of perfection, passion and inspiration must be the chief drivers of the creative process. These passion and inspiration are everywhere and only need the right connection to access and redirect to one's undertakings at any time. Wandering is essential to the creative process. When creative energies are proving illusive, it may be the wandering that connects the creative to the source. And wherever this wander terminates is guaranteed to be unquiet and wondrous.

Wondrous wander

Transforming passion into a work of art, piece of writing, musical compilation and many other forms of creation is naturally laborious. But when such a transformation is a labour of love, the labour is somewhat bearable although not any easier. Those in the know, know that within the great wander that is life, are multiples of wondrous paths. Any one of these paths if traversed committedly, can help stimulate the transformation of deep energy into a finished wondrous object. All it takes is some wandering, undirected and unhinged. This, according to many, is all there is to life. This and knowing that mortals can only create mortal works. The mortality and permanence are not of essence, what matters most is the process of creation. If the objective is to create inspired, passionate works, how these are brought about matters. In explaining the universe, the mother of *wonders* and greatest of all creations, some describe it as a consequence of a great and spectacular big bang. Others suggest the creator went on a long mental wander during which the idea of planets, stars, suns and moons was conceived. This wander, they say is why the creation is wondrous.

An ancient ideology asserts that *Lifachi* (earth) was created by a supreme being, from whom our images were adapted. According to this ideology, the significance of the process humans were created through is evidenced in that we resemble a supreme being. The ideology of *Modimo* asserts that the creation process from which all life is resultant, is the most significant of all processes. On this context, the ideology adds that even a creative mental wandering no matter how undirected, is mighty significant.

Modimo teaches that the product of any creative thought, no matter how random is wondrous. This is the wandering in wonder that many *Modimo* disciples habitually engage during creative moments. Any work created just after or during this wander, is magnificent. This work, whatever it is, it blows one's mind at its simplest; beyond its simplicity, it is simply captivating. It is wondrous.

To many, personal creation is as relevant as nurture to life. Whereas others chase perfection blindly with little regard to perfection's requisites, others get what perfection is about and execute flawlessly. Whereas perfection is an ideal in many respects, a careless want for perfection can be a threat to creativity. Whereas inspired creativity is an avenue to perfection; perfection is not a goal of inspired creativity. Those who have achieved perfection in anything know that perfection can happen when creativity is driven by inspiration and passion. If these are fully transmitted into the creation process, the quality of the work is undeniable, the depth of the finished creation is realisable; and sometimes the perfection of the undertaking also shines through. However, others claim the contrary; that only a strive for perfection is what drives the creative energies into an ultimately perfect creation. They claim that any perfect work is also passionate; that passion is perfection in mystical form. They also claim that perfection can exist in an imperfect form, wherein passion may also thrive. One must maintain an independent and objective thought in such matters. Constantly one is obliged to discard known facts momentarily and lean only on objectivity in order to learn new truths and reach new frontiers. And when one creates anything, one has to trust the inherently perfect nature of the creative process. In most inspired pursuits, perfection permeates the work, it seems almost guaranteed. And, whether one believes in *Modimo* or not, whether one thinks *Lifachi* is a supreme creation or an elaborate chemical reaction; whether the universe was preceded by empty space or a supreme mental wander, one must accept it is wondrous.

The passion invoked on a mental wander for a creative purpose is peculiar, personal and unstealable. Like inspiration, it is available on demand, needing only a relevant state of mind to access it at a given time. At any time, it is but a fire. It may require some spark to ignite its flames occasionally but it must smoulder constantly. One is fortunate if one is able to live off their passions; a life lived this way is a life worth living. If one were to gain any profit at all, it may well be from one's passions. For one to do what one loves and get rewarded in legal tender for it, that is the earthly life. Physical existence does not get better than comfortable living. And whether it is for profit or not, it is always worth doing what one loves. There is always potential for profit if anything is done well. If it is an inspired and passionate creation, its perfection may just be visible to the naked eye. In the meantime, it is only responsible that one tolerates what one does, especially if it affords one some living. This is as important as ensuring that one gets value out of what one does or what one has to do. Of utmost importance is that one engages whenever one gets the opportunity to do what one loves. If one is unsure and stuck, a wander, either physical or mental, may be a good place to start. The physical and mental wandering have been proven to help when the creative energies seem inaccessible or dormant. If undertaken purposefully, either of these wanders is wondrous and significant.

48

Con Fuseus advises to engage beyond the known realm when creating, for therein lies the first significance of any creation.

10. Mess Around

The *Mess Around* celebrates the memories of our late loved ones. The memories recalled in the *Mess Around* are about late siblings, friends and other extended family members. In tribute to them, the piece captures a series of thoughts about a dead brother, his son still struggling to deal with the loss; a former classmate who died too early; a dearly departed sister and what she would be up to if she were alive; the jolly uncle and the cheerful aunt and a friend's mother hopefully resting in the afterlife in peace. Precious moments are not made after loved are dead but any second we share with them while they are alive.

Mess Around

Dedicated to good times, the rare moments; the small windows of time when my head is in the right space and my frame of mind perfectly fits in every detail of every perspective I recall. It is in these moments that given the right company of friends, family or strangers, memories are created. It is in the same moments that in their absence, a *mess-around* with their memories is appropriate. Here is for when the time is just right to recall precious moments.

I do not think his son is grown up yet. I hope he, the son, grows into a responsible young man. I hope he sees the struggle, appreciates the necessity of the hustle and resumes his shift. With him being young and all, he may have a less painful plan; the easy grand plan. His mum had once complained that he was a little complacent. When I got in touch with him, he was a little complainer. I am certain his father would have provided the much needed fatherly push. I know he would have risen to the occasion; he would have liked it too, raising his son. He probably may have been a great dad too. He is my brother.

Confident, hopeful and inspired, she was the reason I went to school most days. As a student, knowing what I was up against if I missed a class was reason to get me off bed. She was my competitor. I used to act like I was her suitor, she liked it. It still saddens me thinking about the professional she could not quite live to be. Although we were young, she seemed to get it, she seemed to feel it when she had to. She was mature, she was emotional, competitive yet respectful. She knew when to acknowledge and when to take a bow. She was easy to talk to, I think this is mostly because she had the rare skill of listening. If angels exist, she is

51

probably mine. If spirits live on, hers is out there. Some lucky young woman has it. She is my friend and former classmate.

I recently confided in a friend that I think about her sometimes, that I wish she were still alive. But then I think about her life path to the day she died; what she had done with herself, what she spent her time doing. Then I decide to not pursue this thought any further. We were good friends she and I. Something tells me that in her last days she had had time to audit her life, and had identified what she would do differently. Only if she had another opportunity; the proverbial *second chance*. Some get many more chances, but some never get too many. She may have had some but she did not have many. I was angry at life because I needed her more around the time she died. Her death hurt but she became my heroine. She believed in me before I did. Only heroic persons have that power and she was certainly one. She is my sister.

Clean shaven, squeaky clean old-school *spects*, well ironed and clean clothes. He wore his shoes shiny and black. They were the government supplied oxfords given to civil servants. They were a decent quality too. He was a night watchman at one of the gates into the town airport runway. He was playful, brutally honest at times and never hesitant to tell someone off. Him and I were okay but not always in good books. I was in Primary school then, had a short temper and was struggling to figure a few things out. I remember him as caring though. He loved his sister, my mother. He was a good man. I hope he is resting in peace-wherever he may be. He is my uncle.

We never spoke about his mother's passing. He never spoke about it. I was careful not to arouse memories of her in whatever I did with him. I thought it was the best way to support a grieving friend. We spoke about everything but just not his mother, or any mother for that matter. She died when he was young, he must have been nine, ten or thereabout. It pained me to even imagine the pain he must felt. He was really close to his mother; he was her only son. She was strict and all but it was not hard to tell that she loved her son deeply. She had done a good job of raising him too. He turned out to be a decent young man, considering what he must have gone through after his mother passed. He moved suburbs a few months after his mum's passing. I have fond memories of him. When we first met, we spoke different languages. He spoke *Kalanga* and I would respond in *Tswana*. This went on for a while until both of us were confident enough to speak the other's language. We remain good friends to date. The memories of the good days we had will take a while to fade as will the memories of his mother. She is my good friend's mother.

I had not seen or spoken with her for more than five years. She and I got along just fine; we just never connected. We had lived and played together at some point in our childhood. I had a good relationship with her mother, my cousin. Her mother's mother, my aunt was a good friend of mine too. I remember that on good days, we used to laugh first and joke after; that's how deep we were, she and I. She was naturally cheerful and talkative. She passed on less than five months after her granddaughter and I had our first conversation in more than five years. Her husband died a few months after she did. I never paid much regard to him. He was ignorant and callous. His wife though, was a good woman. She was a good aunt, as good as an aunt can be.

There are plenty good things to say about my late grandmother, my other late uncle, my late cousin, my late friends Goya and Japi and all my other late friends. This piece is not about their passing, it is about the fond memories we shared. The precious moments I was fortunate to share with them. The more I realise how precious life is, the more I realise that each moment lived counts; that each moment is worth savouring. Many a times, I let go of the truth that none is guaranteed a tomorrow, that all I ever have is the present moment and it is up to me to make it count. It is up to me to turn each moment into a precious memory. These memories are what I recall each time I have some time to *mess around.*

11. Twenty-7 burdens

Twenty-7 burdens is an extract of a journal and describes a journaler's thoughts on dying. The journaler admits to always seeing the future as far as the imagination can go and rarely pondering about death. In the piece, the journaler lists work, rest and play as central parts of the journaler's personal constitution. The journaler describes work as an esteemed and most reliable means of accomplishment. According to *Twenty-7 burdens*, there may be other means to accomplishment including luck but it is the hardworking who usually earn the luck to pick and choose what matters to them.

Twenty-7 burdens

Sometimes I get the naivety of looking into my future, imagining myself as somebody accomplished in some way. Rarely do I take time to imagine my ultimate fate, being dead. But when I do get the rare chance to think about my death, I still imagine that there exists a chance, however *slim,* to beat death in some way. I imagine there is a chance to beat death to some extent or postpone its eventual effect. And so in my naivety I entertain the thought that it must be possible to live just a little longer beyond my physical existence. I also imagine what death feels like, if it is anything like the physical realm, or better. To live, to see the beauty of morning, to err in the craziest of ways, to enjoy some physical encounter and coexist with my fellow. That's my life, I wonder what my death will be like. So I, like many, prefer to live and let my fellow live. This is not a rare attitude. It is as *un-atypical* as wishing that one's causes live a little longer after one dies.

My hope is that when I die, my friend will remember me for a while after I am gone. I wish that my friend recalls on occasion, who I was, my words, my actions to represent these words and my life's work. My enemy equally deserves the opportunity to recall my exploits long after I am dead. I also wish that when I am dead, my family will see just a little clearer what I represented. I wish then that they understand better what I stood for and that each of them also realises what they stand for and what they ought to stand for to be relevant. I hope it is known that I appreciated my peculiarity and individuality and hope you do too; I hope it is known that I stood for our sake and I hope you never forsake it for a selfish sake. Alternate scripts teach that a self that exists independently is

56

particularly vulnerable to the consequences of isolation if this independence is in solitude and in fear. Such selves are doomed to one of two non-favourable fates; deprivation or over-indulgence. Constantly, I work hard to ensure I am not such a self, and that I do not stand for selfish individualism.

At age 27, the time of penning this journal note, my life burdens are almost defined. My yet to be matured mission is to work, rest and play, all of which I think I do well. The work, rest and play ideology is not my original philosophy, but it has taken root in my head from some thought I had consumed in a written piece or a musical compilation. Nevertheless, the philosophy of work, rest and play so far works for me. I have customised the philosophy to suit my situation, I reconfigured the order of terms of the philosophy from work, rest and play to rest, work and play. The motive for reordering the terms will be revealed later. But the reason I adopted the philosophy initially does not extend beyond the common fact that rest is good and essential for good work. Rest enables the regathering of the strengths required for work. I also know that work is an esteemed means to accomplishment. I heard that luck and wealth are other means to a self-defined state of accomplishment. I have come to accept, convinced by readings and personal experiences that sufficient work could earn me all the luck, wealth and charm and everything else I seek to be accomplished. I know also that play is essential. To me, play is about celebrating my existence and that of whoever I play with. My interests and other objects and subjects of play have constantly evolved as I meet new people, learn new things and visit different places but I still play. I believe that when the conditions are right, one must play. This simple attitude is complicated by the conditions on both the play and the player. It is also important to note that excessive play is harmful to any cause and that abuse breaches the rules of noble use. Play requires craft and maintaining craft of play takes attentive vigilance, which can be easily lost in the indulgence of overplay.

Other attitudes I harboured around the time I was 27 include respect, fairness and truth. I have spent time thinking about fairness and have written several times on it. In one of my old writings, I sought to prove that fairness at its depth is similar to the principle of equilibrium and transfer of energy. In the same text, I proposed that world peace, tolerance and universal progress thrive when fairness is at equilibrium. I wrote that it is only when fairness is at equilibrium that anyone accumulates no less than a near exact share of what he or she deserves from their labours and values. I also thought about the idea of truth and what it meant not just to me but o other people. Some of the best writings about truth I found were a couple of texts including the biblical verse that the truth sets one free. The other was a proposition in-vino veritas. The latter text is the theorem I hid behind in my pursuit of the fine fruit of the vine. A good glass of the drink of the gods would make me realise that I did not care too much if my posthumous tribute would not be too long an account. It was also the vino that awoke my need to *self-tribulise*. It was a sudden urgency to pen a précis of who I was at the time and in that moment. In these moments, I would write stories in shorthand, I would paint abstracts with words, I would postulate philosophical theorems. In these moments, I would pen summaries of aspects and realms of life. All these to immortalise my thought and everything else I represented while I lived.

In realising my said naivety on immortality, I acknowledge that my thoughts on living long are only aspirations; the kind that many of us have. I wish to be remembered upon my death, At 27 years of age , I know I do not know it all , that I'm learning through trial and finding my way in my errors. I do however, want it to be known that I do not have enemies. I am aware that some may have considered me their enemy but this did not turn them into my enemies. With the benefit of hindsight, I am appreciative of my upbringing; I am thankful to my mother and grateful of the circumstances and events leading to who I am today. I am proud to have been able to forgive all transgressors and trespassers. Forgiveness has relieved me of a host of burdens, all 27 of them.

If some random reader chanced upon this writing and was privy to the thought of my head, I ask that they imagine that there once lived immeasurable thought in this my head. If they follow and get the meaning of the text, this thought may just catch on and take root in their own head. And when it has taken root in their head, the reader will understand that it is noble to let good thought roam. So I ask of the reader that when I am dead, it is to be known that I let private thought loose. I let it loose in the hope that it spreads good where *little good* existed. I let it loose in the hope that it starts good where good was dead. This is what I stand for and what I wish to be known as having stood for when I am dead.

12. Life Of Death

If Death could communicate, how would it do it? Would she talk? If he could, what would he say? If Death were to materialise physically, what form would it assume? How would death tell its story, what attitude would it have? What kind of interests would an energy like death have if it was a regular being? Would she explain why she kills? Would he relate to the loss that survivors feel when a loved one dies? Would he feel for his victims? Would it regret some of the lives it has taken? The piece of *Life Of Death* assumes the identity of Death and tells its story.

Life Of Death

To those I haven't killed yet, it is only a matter of time.

I live to kill, it is all I do, it is all I am. I kill though a variety of means. I terminate the physical existence of living-things in a number of ways. I am loathed by most. Only a few claim to not hate me. I am mostly feared, a situation I thrive on. Very few admit to not being scared of me. If I don't kill, I might as well be dead so I do what I do; I kill because it is who I am.

I am not sure when I was born. I killed my parents not long after I was born. Some have said I am as old as Life. Some have claimed that the two of us are siblings, Life and I. This is a claim I vehemently dispute. There is no way I could have shared a womb with Life because I would have killed it prenatal. Pregnancy provides an ample enough opportunity to terminate a competitive foetus, especially when it is a matter of Life and Death. Not much is known of my birth, this too is a myth. I am told I started killing very early in my life. My parents were my first victims, shortly after I was born. My closest relatives were next, followed by friends, their closest relatives, their friends and the random stranger that finds themselves on my path. It is for this reason that I have no parents, family and no friends. I have been called names, which I guess I had coming. I have been called heartless; but why would I not have a heart? Must have killed it too. Occasionally, I am labelled ruthless, bad and dangerous; I am known as fatal, the end, the dreaded demise. I don't mind

61

some of the names because they reflect the fear I command. Me and fear go a while back when I was only a child. Apart from instilling fear, I cannot recall much else from my childhood. I hardly remember any dream I ever had except one. In this dream, a dark figure appeared before me and whispered harshly, "There is no escaping you". At first I was scared and terrified by the dark figure. I remember waking up from my dream startled and panting heavily. That was when I met fear. I could not go back to sleep that night. The following night, there it was again, the dark figure and its sharp whisper. This was it, I could not take it anymore. I woke up and have never slept since then, not a single nap, not a blink.

Because I am feared and hated, I only associate with the hopeless and damaged souls, most of whom are already dead. At some point, some thought I was exploitable; they wooed and enticed me. I would kill and they would feast. When it started, there was no deal, no compensation and no favours expected. I just killed because it is what I did. *Gypaetus* salvaged the carcass because it is what he does. The more he stuck around me, the more he realised that it was a matter of time before I killed him. Gradually, he began to keep his distance. Like everyone else, he grew scared of me. But Gypaetus is also uncontrollably greedy and his insatiable greed consistently drowns all his other senses. Repeatedly, Gypaetus would find himself in my presence, sometimes with his good friend *Torgos*. On the odd occasion, to stimulate their fear and greed, I would kill one of their kind. I have always wondered if they realised that we both were who we were and could not help ourselves. To this day, Gypaetus, Torgos and I have this relation of necessity. They associate with me not because they want to but because they are pressed to; it is in their blood. But they also fear me because they know that killing is in my blood.

I assume several forms. Like many enduring phenomena I have had to adapt to ensure my longevity. I endured time, since I came into being I have mastered a million ways to kill. Suicide is not one I created. I never need assistance taking a life. Despite it all, suicide has served me well over the years. Coerced by circumstance, living-things, humans especially have come up with unique ways of ending their lives. Another way I end an existence in the physical world is through disease. I know several lethal diseases and more incurable diseases. Some of these are immediately terminal and will summon me instantly. Whenever I get called I show up, and when I show up something dies. Other diseases instruct that I kill nicely and slowly, usually an organ or system at a time, which ends up being not so nice. In some cases, medicine slows down the disintegration process on the disease struck target, much to my delight. The unfortunate victim endures long episodes of pain and suffering while the medicine buys them a miserable day or two. Ultimately, I interfere and terminate all systems. Oftentimes, I work with an accident, the fatal kind. Most times, my accident victims are careless. Most times when the careless flirt with me, they cause the additional demise of many others whom I initially had no intention of killing, innocent victims. Other tools of my craft include guns; my most reliable of ordnances. As technology advances, so has the precision and *accessorization* of guns. The modern gun is sophisticated; some even accommodate the flaws of a bad shot. Some are small and slim, others are big. Others are programmable and equipped with heat sensors while others are intercontinental and ballistic. Mass murder weaponry certainly contains my massive killing appetite whenever I have one, which is most times. Though my thirst for fatality is rarely quenched, mass killing is surely a treat.

So why do I do it? For a number of reasons. Sometimes I do not ask for it; some of my victims should not have died had either they or someone else taken the appropriate precaution, listened and understood, accepted and tolerated, not acted on selfishness, thought it through and done the right thing. I obviously thrive on the error, selfishness, fallibility and weakness of most of my victims. Strangely, I rarely cringe every time I have to kill; I only hesitate very briefly if I have to kill an innocent victim. Fortunately for me, my job is complete as soon as a body is dead; I never have to stick around for the aftermath. I also guess that I do what I do because I was born deadly, it is who I am, it is what I do, it is in my blood, I am good at it, nobody and nothing else does what I do. I am a part of life, no one has ever fully lived until they are dead. I have met a few who were not scared of me, I could tell they had fully lived and were ready to move on to whatever was next for them. These, I kill with respect because I respect a life fully lived. Any life lived fully is always ended gallantly. This is the only value I observe. This is also the only time I get to meet a contented living-thing, all others that I kill are scared, sad, bitter, regretful, and unhappy. When I kill them, the unhappy kind, I have hope. I hope that they get it in their next phase; whatever it is they could not find while they were living.

Despite *dis-appearances* of those I kill, I am not scared of being me. I get to experience beauty, passion, frustration, disappointment, relief, fright and the many other emotions. I get these experiences through the living-things I have the monopolised opportunity

64

to kill. Occasionally I get to be amused as well. Once in a while, I also get shocked by the poor life who turns religious at the moment of their death. Out of panic, many appeal to the supreme, asking for mercy, forgiveness and the lot. It is usually too late because I proceed with a kill despite the supreme appeal. Infrequently, I laugh at them. It is a laughter I have to have, if I do not laugh at them, then I will never laugh at all. Laughter is a rarity when you kill for a living.

13. Afro-graphics

Any informed person anywhere in the world must be aware of the significant imbalance in the living conditions of Africa relative to the rest of the world. The significance of this obvious disparity is evident between the rich and poor, not just the African poor but the world's poor people. *Afro-graphics* is the unofficial and untypical, literary and graphic atlas of Africa. The piece is structured around subtle titles capturing some aspect of the land and people of Africa. The piece commemorates the good and weeps at the bad of Africa. For instance, the section titled *Fashion show* profiles the variety of tradition and the breadth of African culture in terms of dressing. The commentary of *Afro-graphics* is a personal take.

Thought unstructured

The typical story is often logical and follows some chronology. Such a story usually has an intended moral; love, hate, the power of good, forgiveness, evil and others. The purpose of the described story may be to entertain, educate, remind, scare and a host of other predetermined intentions. The following is not a typical story. It is a direct translation of random thoughts about the vast phenomenon that is Africa. The moral of this unstructured thought is not definitive either. Relevant conclusions will be drawn according to personal understandings and perceptions of the story. This is not unusual for untypical stories.

Cradle of Mankind

The weather is bad; really bad. The climate has become cruel. It has been so for a while now. It has been practically impossible to attain self-sufficiency in crop production or food security as it is known in some circles. It makes sense too; it makes sense to attach security to one's food production and supply. Lately it has been speculated in a number of forums that the next big war will be over food. However, this is another matter, another topic. The matter at hand is that climate change has not just incapacitated the ability to self-provide but has also crippled the economy. This is usually the precursor to lawlessness, from small scale looting to petty crime and to the more heinous and more lucrative level of corruption. Although climate change is not the sole cause of the said evils, it is doing its part of the damage and must be rightly acknowledged or adequately condemned. This notorious change in climatic patterns is affecting every living-thing within its reach, and this is the entire earth. Because of climate change, evolutions that traditionally took years and generations of species have become instant. Research reports that families of plants and animals with known traits have displayed completely opposite behaviour patterns within weeks. Scientific observers reported that the usually harmless pigeon was recently observed showing unusual characteristics of aggression to humans. Theorists have proposed a connection of this unbecoming behaviour to the rapidly changing climate. It is a logical proposal given the state of affairs.

Gifted offspring

She was always content. This is the most distinguished trait about her. How could she not be? She had given birth to some of the most remarkable personalities in that generation, this generation and the next. One of her sons was Rolitrii. He represented resilience, consciousness, and was a model for leadership. Roli has become known and respected worldwide for his convictions. To his siblings, he became an excuse for progressive ambition and the reason not to lack such ambition. The rest of Africa's children include some of the finest sportsmen, celebrated entertainers and a good supply of the West's doctors, accountants and other white, blue and grey collar labour troops. At some point the commander in chief of the most powerful army in the world and executive overseer of the largest economy in the world was a grandson of Africa. One of Africa's sons had fathered him while he was overseas to attain some educational qualification. Western education has been both a gift and curse to Africa. However, the general belief is that there is a stronger case for the good that education has brought and continues to bring to Africa. Some of these benefits include organised governments, however corrupt; educated civil societies, however uninformed;

68

and established institutions, however ineffective. The same benefits are also regularly cited as attributes of a developed people. The other reported ingredient of a developed people is leadership. It is this leadership that had also been reported as scarce in the land of Africa. This allegation is probably false but a series of frequently telecasted evidence validates this opinion. The other potentially undisputable opinion is that Africa has in her loins and in existence, offspring of the calibre of the reported leader. In this case too, ample existing evidence supports this opinion. Africa does have the gifted offspring but sadly, as in any other family, there exists the pathetic black sheep. Gamu, another son of Africa, was one such sheep.

Brain drought, a natural selection

The theory of survival of the fittest is such that the strongest species outsmarts, outplays, outworks, out-produces and ultimately outlives and out-survives its fellows. Evolutionists propose that this is essentially the process that resulted in the extinction of the *homo-erectus* and the emergence of the self-titled modern-man, the homo-sapien. Apparently this same theory, the theory of survival of the fittest is in play in the modern world. The theory of survival of the fittest postulates that as resources become scarce in a given habitat, the resultant species is one that must have somehow out-manoeuvred its fellow cohabitants. Although the idea of out-manoeuvring fellow beings may seem gratifying for the fittest survivor, it also turns life into a competition and depicts mass existence as unsustainable. The proposed winner in the great contest of life according to this theory is the strongest, smartest, most enduring, hardest working and otherwise superlative being. This makes sense given the context of limited resources but the fittest survivor is also the most unfortunate because he faces the fiercest conditions in his depleted habitat. She is also lonely and on constant alert from a competitive neighbour. Ultimately he leads an empty life, assuming that purpose matters to him. So in the long run, this game has no winners because even the last woman standing succumbs. In economic conspiracies, it has been proposed that the stronger economies will outlive and possibly consume the smaller economies. In recent decades, there has been an alarming mass movement of skilled and active manpower out of Africa. Those who can, do leave Africa, most of them for good and for good reason. Alternative history has it in good record that this exodus is much greater than one that hit ancient Egypt in the times of the Pharaohs when Moses led multitudes of the Egyptian labour force out to the promised land. It might not have been economically viable to the Egyptian government back then and it is definitely not viable for Africa's economy. To date, many of African economies have virtually zero professional capability because most of the able bodied in this respect have fled to greener pastures. Fleeing is only a human instinct in any case and is usually preferable over the much harder alternative, staying. Some stayers in this context have the will and means to flee but pledge to hold the fort, come what may. The flyers in this case should not be chastised because some stayers wish they could also flee. They are forced to stay because they have not the means to flee. Apparently, this is the theory of survival of the fittest at play in our modern world. The superior thrive and live longer while the weak gradually disappear. The rules have not changed.

Evening newscast

Every weekday between 5 and 7 pm in any given time zone, most television stations broadcast the day's news bulletin. A number of common events have consistently featured in the international news of late. In Mogadishu, Somalia, a group of armed rebels have dissolved government and practically defeated the national armed forces. Thousands are displaced and harassed. In Ethiopia's capital Addis Ababa, the story of hunger and starvation is all too common. With multitudes of infants eradicated, despair is visible in people's faces. Further south towards the Kalahari in Gaborone Botswana, the human immunodeficiency virus is pandemic. The already small nation is losing generations of young and old alike and AIDS is only worsening the situation. To the east of Botswana, is better known Zimbabwe. Harare and Bulawayo are well drained of their professional labour pool and many more people continue to want out and get out of the country. The local currency is worthless; the foreign dollar is the most relevant legal tender in these parts of town. To the north of Africa in Cairo Egypt, a power vacuum has been declared and chaos is being televised. The looting of worthless ancient Egyptian artefacts in museums, described by many as rife, is robbing the country of its national heritage. In Lagos Nigeria, corruption and poverty are trending. Private small armies threaten the supply of oil, the country's main resource and source of revenue. Youth unemployment and disenchantment with the authorities is widespread; not just here but elsewhere in Africa. The telecast of these news items is vivid. The apparent hopelessness of the victims is never lost in transmission. Meanwhile to some, this telecast is reality. It is not as painful as viewers perceive it from a TV screen. It is much more; and it will last much longer after the evening newscast has concluded.

The Fashion show

Sandstorms, hot days and cold nights; these are just typical features. Welcome to the Sahara. Some Arabia live here in this desert they call the *Sa'hra*. The Bantu are the natives of this land and happily coexist with other visiting tribes. The dress code in this territory is robe; around the face, around each leg, around both upper legs and over the upper body. Shaving is for the less understanding here. The norm is to let the hair grow; the longer of it one has, the more connected to high powers one is perceived to be. For some of the women, the long hair represents beauty while for men, a long beard signifies wisdom. The sophisticated dude wears a snow white set of robes and smokes a shisha when he is chilling. To the eastern tropics, around Kenya and Tanzania; the gear of choice is the *Shuka*. This is a piece of cloth worn in some sophisticated manner often exposing one of the shoulders of the usually slim and tall Maasai. The respected colours are bright yellow and red. A typical catwalk in these lands would feature a tall, young woman with a shaved head and defined facial features. Her earrings are larger than her ears. She is wearing a long, red cloth. It is not as plain and boring as it appears at first sight. This is abstraction at play; the simple looking outfit has a story behind it. Understanding this story unravels the sophistication behind the simple. To the south, near the *Kgarari* also known as the Kalahari of Botswana; if underground minerals could shine through the surface, the Kalahari would be the most sparkly spot on earth. Many a *krafuta* has been mined in this land. In the Kalahari, leather is truth in fashion terms. The San roam this land and have done so for years. The San is who the Texan cowboy aspires to be, a self-sustaining, carrying no gun and keeping no livestock, yet sufficiently safe and has a good supply of meat, root and berry. The San man rocks a leather *budgy-smuggler*, smokes herbs and is completely nomad. The typical man about town rocks older, vintage and softer leather *budgies*, the latest design includes a small pocket for herbs and charms. His hair is short and unkempt-like but authentic and elegant. The hippier of the lot habitually wears locally crafted bracelets, a few in each wrist. These are just a few of the exhibits in the African fashion show. The just described range of dress codes is not all there is in the vast land of Africa. The scenarios outlined only tell a small part of a bigger story. The actual encounters usually captivate more than the wildest imagination. Such is the depth of the African couture. Such is the breadth of the scenery in Africa's cultural landscape. If it's sentimental it's sexy because in this affair, sentiment is the currency of choice.

Strength in struggle, the long walk

Some law of nature asserts that what goes around comes around. To some, what this law teaches is that in the long run, balance prevails. To some, this law encourages endurance. And to some, this law wakes the idea of hope and expectation; the hope that the small strides being continually made eventually amount to the giant leap desperately needed. The workings of nature are seldom precisely understood. But as long as nature plays by the law of eventual balance, then what is to be will be. In an imperfect world, even the small chance seems like too much of an ask given that fairness is irrelevant. It is for this reason that the yearning for the eventual appeals just a little more than the next best grand plan. And those involved in any sort of grand plan deserve accolade. Their efforts will not go unnoticed. This way, their struggles would not have been in vain. It is in struggle that strength is extracted; the strength needed to carry-on when physical resources run into depletion; this struggle is the source of the motivation required to keep at it when inspiration is dwindling. And so it is thanks to the law of nature, for it provides the reason to be hopeful, to appreciate each step taken in the struggle. For everyday living, the law of nature gives reason to discard negativity and smile from one's depths. The law of nature enables one to be grateful for their given space and time. This law of nature provides inspiration to many; the many that find the strength to live when death surrounds them. The many who have reason to be sceptical and apprehensive of tomorrow yet look forward to it anyhow; the *have-nots*, the many who can only give immaterially. They own not an item yet continue to give generously.

14. If I got

Each piece of Abstraxion attempts to maintain a certain energy. The piece of *If I got* is meant to have a romantic energy. It is a shorthand about a friend, a partner, a lover and soul mate. If I got a friend so dear, a friend so true, a friend such as you, I would count myself lucky. Here is to good friends.

If I got

If I got a friend so dear,
a friend so true.
If I got a friend such as you,
I would count myself lucky.
And if I got such luck,
I would hold on for *dear-ever*.

If I got a partner so faithful,
a partner so loyal.
If I got a partner like yourself,
I would consider myself prosperous.
And if such prosperity was mine,
I would appreciate it every passing day.

If I got a soulmate so whole,
a soulmate so content.
If I got a soulmate like you,
I would be constantly stoked.
And if I got stoked by you,
I would surely shine brighter.

If I got a life with you,
A life so accomplished, a life so fulfilled.
If I got through life with you,
I would call myself successful.
And if I amassed such success,
would I share it?
There's no way I would share you.

If I got a lover so passionate,
A lover so ardent.
If I got a lover like you,
I would spare a thought for Atamu,
And if you were my Eifa,
I would happily partake of your fruit.

So if I got successful and accomplished,
And got a life with you.
And if I was prosperous and constantly stoked,
because of a soulmate such as you,
I would declare myself fortunate.
Now that I have such fortune,
I have a life worth living.

15. Fur meine Likle

This piece is inspired by Beethoven's *Fur Elise*. The piece acknowledges that there can be no worthier reason to be in love other than for love itself. When this piece was penned, the writer imagined the mindset of a composer in the process of composing a timeless classic on love. The piece is composed on the idea that less is more and that simple is sophisticated. Like *Fur Elise*, this is for my *Likle*.

Fur meine Likle

Apparently we have only just met. According to some innuendo, I have barely had the time to know you. Apparently there is more to you than just the infectious smile. According to some conspiracy, you are nowhere near who I think you are. Apparently you are not the unassuming friend I spend every weekend with, that is what they say.

We are different, indigenous Rhodesian and *Chuana;* our cultures cannot mix. We are incompatible. We do not even match; you being tall and me being not. This is what they say. Our family will not have an identity. Our children will not self-discover. We do not have a home. We are too different to have a home. This is what they say too.

Who cares what they say? Not me. It bothers me not that they say things. Things that don't build us; things that highlight the disparities and not the similarities between us; things that expose the naivety in us. They say many things; all of which are unconstructive. They wait for the day they may say *they told us so.* But who cares? *Mich nicht.*

We fell in love, or whatever this thing we are in is. We started as fellows from the motherland, then evolved to brother and sister, then friends, then upgraded to a beneficiary friendship, then we became lovers and ultimately professed love for one another. We have had the bad days, we still do. We have had good days, we still savour them. What a thing we have, you and I. That we chanced upon and fell into it only adds to the mystique of it.

79

I love you. I believe I do, my thoughts and feelings validate it. I love the way you look when you laugh. I love that heartfelt smile you dissipate when you are delighted. I love the way you tell me I'm great. I love the way we dream together- a perfect life. I don't like it when we fight, but love it when we make up before the end of the day and wind up kissed up, loved up and ready to rock it where the hell ever.

Our love is bigger than us. This is what we agreed to, that our love is bigger than anyone of us. None of us is perfect, none of is flawless. We err, we fault, we disappoint, we embarrass. Yet we stand ready to defend our love. We look out for one another. We watch each other's backs. We support one another. Through thick fog, we find one another. Through thin openings, we wriggle through for each other.

With you I have grown. With you I have seen places. With you, I have suffered losses. With you I have struggled. With you I have endured pain. With you I have cried. With you I have laughed. With you I have enjoyed bliss. With you I have conquered. With you I have won victories. With you I have met love, accepted love and lived in love. With you I continue to grow.

The future is uncertain. If sometime in the future, our love is no more; either by design or accident, I wish it known that it was love we were after. It was love we got in it for. It was love we were trying to be in. It was love that got us this far. It was love that got us this close. It was love that got us all we had. Yes we hustled some. But we hustled for us, we hustled for one another, we hustled for love. The future may be uncertain, but our love is now. And now, we are in love.

Loving you is an opportunity. Loving you is an honour. Loving you is a privilege. Loving you keeps me off trouble. Loving you fulfils me. Loving you is demanding. Loving you is a responsibility. Loving you is a full time job. Loving you is determined. Loving you is not all knowing. Loving you is trying. Loving you is conscious. Loving you is keen to keep you. Loving you is the biggest thing I have ever done. Loving you is what I do every day. And I get the opportunity to do it exclusively for you. Loving you is my pleasure.

16. Nurturing the Dream

This is a summary of another one of my journal notes, originally written on 26 January 2011. The journal notes were written as introspection on some aspects of my life in Australia. It was an overdue acknowledgement of all I had learnt and experienced in Australia. Australia had presented me with numerous opportunities and I wrote *Nurturing the Dream* as homage to the land and the people of Australia. In my journal notes, I briefly describe the typical trip of adequate ambition. I write that for any adequate ambition, if the effort is constantly worth the challenge, then the trip of achieving ambition is *bloody awesome*. Daring to dream and chasing after the dream is no small feat, not if one is too familiar with the frequent failures of life. *Nurturing the Dream* details the challenge that is the dream, and the challenge of nurturing the dream. This dreamer welcomes the attitude that constantly awakens him to himself; he knows where he is been, he knows where is at and he knows precisely where he is headed.

Nurturing the Dream

That day in 2011 on 26 January, like many in Australia, I paused and thought of the many things I was grateful of about Australia. I started my notes by acknowledging and thanking the *Wathauring* and *Wurrundjeri* peoples as traditional landowners of my place of residence and work. I also acknowledged elders past and present of all the indigenous peoples of Australia.

Australia had become my second home over the years. I had amassed a fair bit of knowledge, experience and a certain wisdom from this land. It was in Australia that I had learnt many things that had mattered to me greatly at various points in my life. Whether these matters sustained their relevance is a matter for another day. The day of 26 January however, matters to many in Australia. So as a guest of the people of Australia, I felt a certain obligation to express some personal gratitude. I penned a piece that day on nurturing dreams and specifically, nurturing my own dream. I emphasised the importance of staying the course of one's dream, no matter how rugged the terrain. I also noted a sensation of the growing pressures of my own dream, its' ever hardening challenges and a seemingly continuing elusiveness. I also noted how I occasionally paused to reaffirm my causes. I noted that I had discovered for myself that it was of no benefit to me to fight personally irrelevant causes. I *self-advised* that a just cause is a mutually beneficial cause. Beneficial to me and my neighbour, and his neighbour too if it matters to their cause.

I recorded that I had occasionally stolen a couple of moments to rethink my priorities and readjust ambitions. I suspect most people do. Most of the time on such occasions, I would resolve to resume and plough on the original course, the original dream. I would remind myself that I had found a purpose and it worked just right. I wrote that this purpose may be challenging most times, usually deep and risky sometimes, fun almost all the time, inspired whenever possible and occasionally overwhelming. In my notes, I wrote of a need to specify this dream for the sake of one of my *27 burdens* but I resolved that this personal dream had to stay personal. Repeatedly, at different parts of the journal note, I wrote about the urge to reveal details of my dream but consistently resisted the urge. Buoyed by a sudden feeling of self-worth, I declared in my notes that although it seemed simple, my dream was anything but. I noted that I knew that my dream was revolutionary. I noted that it may not be televised, may not even materialise but my revolution would surely be pursued with endless vigour.

I wrote that my dream may not be popular but it is the common dream, the other guy's dream. I also added that the commonality of my dream did not compromise its quality. It enhanced it, if anything. The dream was not small, it had never been small, not at any time of its existence. It was conceived big, which is why pursuing it was an accomplishment in itself. I wrote that my success unravels with every ounce of energy I redirect to my dream, with each minute I spend in the process of pursuing it. I acknowledged that at times it felt impossible, too mythical and unconquerable. I also accepted that I constantly feel the pressure of maintaining the physical, emotional and spiritual vigour required in chasing dreams as big as I had. I described the sneaky moments of self-doubt which at the time I had managed to consistently dispel rather promptly every time. I described the confusions I fell into on occasion and wrote that in spite of confusion, it was my purpose to pursue my dream. I described how sometimes it felt like I had chosen the harder cause and dreamt the impossible dream. In one line I wrote, 'As glorious as it is to have the audacity to dream, it is vital also, to be awake to the challenge of nurturing the grand dream, if it is grand'.

In one part of my notes, I wrote that when motivation runs low, it may be helpful to look to past glories and reignite the sparks that activated me then. I recalled several moments when *crude will* took me through seemingly impossible hurdles. I also suggested that these moments may be the heart of why I do it, why I bother to think the impossible, to be turned naïve and be made foolish by my imaginations. I also wrote against wandering aimlessly at irrelevant causes. I wrote that it was painful to pursue matters irrelevant to one's conceived purpose. I also expressed concern about leading a causeless life and hoping it would lead to some *destination-worthwhile*. To this concern, I wrote that a cause consistently pursued will always be worthy of the destination, if there is any to be reached. I acknowledged that some destinations seemed better than others, but this was only according to a personal definition of good and better. I wrote that I believed that the best destiny is a self-determined one.

I dedicated a few lines of my journal notes to gratefulness, I recorded that I was grateful that I had a cause and renewed my commitment to my causes. I noted that although some things that do not kill also terribly weaken, it is still worthwhile being weak from a fight than being strong in hiding. I wrote that it is weakness wherein strength is harnessed. I wrote a note of encouragement that we; all who harbour dreams shall wait and get our strengths renewed, that we run and not be weary and walk and not grow faint. I accepted that many worthy dreams are a long walk and wrote that I prayed for the continued sustenance of all dreams to live their dreams. I advocated for self-motivation and that it must be *habitualised* and maintained and that it must inspire those in need of it. I also noted my occasional self-audit was working for me. I wrote that the occasional self-examination of self by self was a commendable exercise. I counselled that nothing should be feared from a *self-mirroring* exercise and that if there are personal issues to be discovered through a self-audit then so be it.

I concluded my journal entry of 26 January 2011 with a note that my fears must also be my motivators; that my fears must be a reminder of why I am worth it. On my fear of failure and fear of loss; I wrote that they must at least remind me to pay relevant dues to what I stand for. They must activate me to contribute sufficient energies to my labours. I wrote that in many contexts, fear is a negative but is equally appropriate as a positive stimulant. I wrote that I personally welcomed fear as a stimulant; that I occasionally ran into fear but always know it gets better in the long run, which is why had I kept running.

17. Leverage

Most of the pieces of Abstraxion were decided upon in the moment. Consequently, they are representations of the writer's state of mind at different times. The deliberation of *Leverage* is no different. It captures the writer's circumstance at the time. *Leverage* is an abstract on reality, integrity and pride. It was written for solace and release. It was written to encourage endurance at a difficult time. The introductory note declares that the piece is an abstraction of actual events happening at the time of the writing. The piece advises that in estimating individual leverages, care must be taken to not underestimate the leverage of others. The piece proposes that the leverage of others must be considered uncertain, must be respected and must mark a readiness to up the personal ante if need be. *Leverage* notes that for the *selflessly selfish* advancement of the unrepresented, it is important that the cause of men be placed above and over the cause of the man.

Leverage

The inquisition on *Leverage* was borne when one was experiencing hardship. Having to endure a string of difficult events, one was forced into a corner. Forced into a corner, one had to do what one does best, strategise. Wrestling with bitter emotion, knowing that the time to act was overdue, one was found without an action plan. Struggling to contain rage, one had to assess their leverage against that of the opposing force. In objectively assessing the said leverages, one ensured that the anger and desperation felt did not affect the objectivity of the undertaking. Instead, the anger and stubborn persistence were redirected into the deep energies needed to complete the task at hand, plan an overwhelming move.

At the time, a number of hateful events had left one with a need to recount and recall all of one's measures of leverage; what one was worth, financially, morally, emotionally and socially; in cash and in kind. One decided that one's strongest leverage at the time was the sense of calculation, the ability to extrapolate and see ahead of time. One was best suited to calculate and connive, to camouflage if forced into the corner of compromise. One's instinct suggested an immediate retaliatory action but one decided that instinct was only needed in doses at the time. One decided on calculated choreography, a particular pattern of aggressive and evasive steps. Like a drunken kungfu master, one decided to dance with lethal moves. It had to be brainstormed and planned. Emotions ran high, instinct dictated a noisy uprising but the sense of calculation prevailed. The strategy collated one's individual leverages in concentration. The resulting explosive could only be used once so timing had to be precise.

Either by choice or chance or a particular compromise of one's patience, one is bound to pounce if continuously prodded. When the fragile equilibrium between humanity and animalism is rocked, man can easily turn animal. Such is the stuff man is made of and how man was made to operate. It may well be fate too. When one prods the other, when a man transgresses another man, the leverages of their individual fates determine who between transgressor and defender triumphs. When one is forced to recount their leverage against an opposing leverage, it helps if one knows who they are, what they have destined themselves for, what they were made for and what they will fight for. These are the elements of one's leverage. Together with strength and will, these self-determined fates are critical to one's leverage. It matters how one perceives them, it is important how one harbours, dispenses and deploys them. The way one calculates their individual leverage is vital.

When determining one's leverage, one needs to consider all avenues of potential available to one including both seen and unseen worth, hard cash and soft virtue, latent and spiritual energy, material and invested value, physical and mental strength. All capitals, whether be they political, financial or social, must be counted. One must consult and instantly decide on the counsel of instinct. Additionally, one must consider the fourth dimension, one's sixth sense, one's capability for additional sensory perception. The aggregation of these into readily dispensable power is one's leverage. When this leverage is calibrated against the worth of another, one must assume the foe possess a certain level of leverage. The specific measure of the foe's leverage is uncertain and this uncertainty must command respect but not fear for the foe.

Whatever degree it may stretch to, the leverage of the foe must not be feared. The uncertainty of the measure of the opponent's leverage demands a constant readiness to up ante if required, a continuous preparedness to shield one's liberties. The uncertainty in another man's leverage must be catalyst to one's efforts in harnessing more strength, skilling up, working harder, optimising resource efficiency and holistically getting better. The uncertainty must activate within one's mind, a precise balance of patience and instinctive response. One must know when to cede to the prompts of instinct and when to lie still, in wait for the right time to strike. No matter how much leverage he may seem to harbour, the foe must not be feared, especially when he is the aggressor. The uncertainty of the leverage of the foe must stimulate the energy of a short sprint and the endurance of a long run. One must be sensitive to the defence of their shortcomings and the exploitation of their strengths. Whatever the circumstance, leverage may only be spent in defending the potential of or effecting great impact. It must be nurtured for the *selflessly-selfish* advancement of the unrepresented, for the cause of men over and above the cause of a man, even if the man is a good man. Leverage must be retained for the pursuit of good and better, bigger and greater.

Initially uncertain, dog suddenly stops whining and hanging his tongue off his mouth, momentarily he runs his tongue across his teeth, they are sharper than ever, he knows what's at stake if he doesn't bite back; he feels the strength of his wagging tail, He growls and barks quietly to hisself. He is about to tear a cat up.

18. The man, The good man

This piece celebrates everything that is good about the good man. He is inherently good, he was born of good. He acknowledges that the goodness of the fellow good man has also helped him become good. This is a piece for good men. Keep up the good work, it is not easy to stay good but it is good being a good man. No matter how much temptation he runs into and succumbs to, if he never forgets the good he is worth to those he lives around, there is a good chance he is a good man.

The man, the good man

The man is a good man, inherently. Born of good, conceived by good people, he is good, has to be good. A good baby at birth, he had the features expected of a good baby. He had a good upbringing, was raised and bred good. Thriving in the good raising, the good baby grew into a good toddler, and toddled well into a good boy. When he started school, the good boy made a good pupil. At his peak he was beyond good, he was excellent, his good teachers called him brilliant. Consistently on good marks, the good pupil cum good student graduated with grades beyond good. The good student excelled and maintained good standards; he enrolled in tertiary classes and became a good scholar; he aspired and acquired good titles; *cum laude* bachelor with honours and doctor of philosophy. Why not if not, the good scholar's motto. His good mother paid not a good cent for the university honours and the *philosophication* of the good son. Instead, the good work she invested in instilling into her good son the good principles earned the good scholarships; gestures of good corporate social responsibility.

The good boy once met a girl. There was no evidence then to determine the goodness or lack of from this hopefully good girl. Good times later, it turned out she was a good girl. In fact, this good girl developed into a good friend to the good boy. The two enjoyed a good friendship for a good while. For this good while the good girl was a good lady friend and a good lover to the good boy. She gave the good boy some good attention on a good, regular basis. She had good plans, worked hard for them too, which made her a good candidate for a good partner. The good duo decided to socialize and formalize their good union. It is no surprise that the good man ultimately decided it was time to be a good boyfriend, commissioned good jewellers and engaged the good girl with a goodly sized rock. At the altar, he pledged to be a good husband. The good man agreed to a good contract of holy matrimony. Guests at the good ceremony confessed it was like none they had been to, ever. They said there was no doubt that whatever the good bride saw in the good groom was good. The good man appreciated his good wife, adored his good wife and understood that not all good boys get the good girls.

The good man hopes to father a good son or good daughter. There is enough good old dirty bustards as it is. The good man intends to raise his good family well, to teach them good and promote good fights. The good father will watch them grow into good, soulful people, make good use of the good times and exploit good opportunities. The good man hopes also that his good children meet good people, one of whom may well become a good partner, a good spouse possibly. They may not seem good at first encounter but can be stimulated into good lovers, good friends and good everything else. Such is the hope; that the next good generation thrives for the survival of the following good generation. Such is the wish; that the good children bear good grandchildren; and that the good grandchildren bear good great grandchildren, grand children to the good children. The great grandchildren will also be bred good; hopefully upholding the good philosophies of their good great gran, the good man.

The good man endeavours to live and lead a good life. This good life is to be lived anywhere where good thrives. Eating good food and sipping good spirits whenever he affords to, the good man thinks the good thought and has good guilty pleasures. He has heard of good wishes not being horses, and has it on good authority that good coincidences favour a certain good people; the prepared. He understands that the good life demands good work, and that to work good means doing it smart whenever possible and hard whenever necessary. In tiredness, the good man rests and appreciates the goodness of a good breather. The good rest always follows the completion of some good work. In his acquaintances, the good man keeps and endeavours to maintain company with the good bunch, the dependable kind. Good company is a pleasure to the good man; his good friends bring good energy.

To his good neighbour, the good man returns good, swears by the good old 'do unto others' ideal. He does to them the good he hopes they do unto him. Such is the way of the good man. Acknowledging that it is not always a good world, the good man wishes that the little good there is to be found should be found by all. And so in anticipation of the reality of his good dream, conscious to the fragility of the good life, in good respect of the foe's leverage and in reverence of the good man's own power and might; the good man plays it good, lives a good life, strives to be good, to do good and stay good.

To age gracefully; the good man's desire. Inspired to do just that, the good man commits to learning; learns good philosophies and recalls good teachings. Borne of good, raised on good thought and taught good manners; the good man is about the goodness of things. Born a good boy and now a good man; past his good lover, good husband, good father, good affair and good great gran days; he will die a good man. Generation of generation will know that great-great gran was a good gran to their good gran, and that

94

above all he was not just any man, he was The man, The good man.

19. The Mystique of Umaru

What and who Umaru is, is a subject of deep divisions in history literature. A number of old mythologies suggest that Uh'Maruh was a common 5th century name. Others propose that Umaru was a powerful 10th century ruler. Many others argue that 'The Umaru' was a title or a set of entitlements awarded to certain individuals in the old world. Other literatures present Umaru as a mythical figure, usually representing some spirit. In terms of what the name means and whether there is a significance to it, some sources assert that Umaru is an early BC word describing a circular object. Some have suggested that *Umaru* literally means infinity and many others advise that the word *Umaru*, means 'together forever' or 'whole'. It is still not known why most recorded accounts agree substantially on this point yet differ so much on all other aspects of Umaru. The *Mystique of Umaru* summarises some of the many historical myths and propositions written about Umaru.

The Mystique of Umaru

Believed to be born on the twelfth day of the second century before Christ, no literature has a decisive timestamp of his birthday. Most writings however, agree that his birthday was the twelfth day, sometime in 2 BC. Some source claim he was born to a poor single mother, others allege that he was born to an ancient BC nobility. A 4th century text titled *Mundo Historius* asserts that on that day was born Umaru, the last of eight siblings. Others claim he had more siblings than eight. Not much is said or written about his siblings; who they were, what they did or their interaction with their younger brother Umaru. However, some late second century records report of a close relationship between Umaru and his family.

In his childhood, Umaru is alleged to not have had, nor needed much to play with. Instead, he took to perusing through a range of scrolls he had access to at his home. At age six, Umaru could read and write, a rarity at the time. Throughout his life, he is believed to have constantly quoted the first century book of *Setho-* a text on the essence of being. Setho was written in the ancient language of *Botho*. It is believed that *Botho* is one of the original BC languages and was widely spoken around the world for at least 60 centuries. For this reason, many early and mid BC philosophical writings use the word 'Botho' as a representation of a set of values and not only a language. The fewer books that attempt to decrypt the ancient language conclude that the vocabulary of *Botho* was somewhat narrow in terms of spoken words but significantly vast in meanings. Respected authorities in 2 BC literature including the grand philosopher Con Fuseus have written that the language of Botho was a guiding principle on people's interactions at the time. Thus Botho was termed the language of life and nature. This is also why most philosophies regard *Botho* not just as a language but a way of life. Because of his fluency in the language and ideas of Botho, many written accounts report that Umaru was au fait in several subjects on life.

Records on the life of Umaru are contradictory. Many think that Umaru was meticulously private, but others have pinioned that he must have always been surrounded by layers of loyal guardians and minders. Proponents of the latter thesis also believe that Umaru was born to a *societally-significant* family. The same explain that the access to the finest schooling evident through his elaborate writings meant that Umaru was born with a stone spoon in his mouth. Others reject this proposition and argue that Umaru's texts on personal revolution justifies that he was himself a simple man, a man with nothing and after everything. The great confusion on who Umaru was has given rise to the idea that 'Umaru' might not have been just a single individual but a title, bestowed to select individuals. Most 3 – 15 BC literature suggest that Umaru was a title, not a name. There is an additional host of writings commonly agreeing on the nature of this title. In a 3 BC encyclopaedia, Umaru is described as a title to which only a few were bestowed based on a number of qualities peculiar only to them. Those who posit that Umaru was a title, add that all read text at the time could only be written or sanctioned by any individual with the Umaru title. Two 5 BC philosophies discovered in separate continents concur that 'The Umaru' was a title, a set of entitlements. However, a 7 BC mythology advises that the U'Maru spirit was governed by a higher power and inspired only on individuals selected by this higher power. According to this mythology, the Umaru was a spirit who only spoke abstractly through a group of spiritual scribes.

For all the literature that agree that Umaru was the name of an individual, there is great discord in their contradictory descriptions on the character of this Umaru. For example some argue that Umaru went about exploiting his nobility entitlements and profiting illegally from the sacred knowledge that was only meant for nobles. Other texts declare that Umaru was passionate of his duties and was dedicated to his responsibilities, which is why he became the most celebrated of ancient nobles. In either literature or mythology, the presentation of Umaru as a defiant individual is interestingly unanimous. A point of agreement is that whether wealthy or impoverished, noble or humble, Umaru defied his class. This depiction of Umaru seems to have survived centuries of rewritings and retellings of his legend. All known drawings and paintings of Umaru by notable 6 BC impressionists and 40 AD artists portray Umaru in valiant light. Strangely, only two poems are known to have been written directly about Umaru. One of the poems is neither critical nor sympathetic of Umaru but the other praises his persistence and acknowledges his will. Some conspiracists question the language structure in the latter poem and suggest that it was written by Umaru himself. They claim that the particular use of the *Botho* diction in the poem matches that in other texts thought to have been authored by Umaru.

The reason most early BC texts constantly refer to an Umaru or quote *The Umaru* increases the confusion about Umaru. In an attempt to decipher the identity of

Umaru, to define whether Umaru was a spirit, a title, one individual or a name representing several individuals; there have been numerous newer explanations. A host of translated commentaries on the Book of Thoth claim that the original text of Thoth referred constantly to some 'Umaryu'. Although a handful of historians and scholars question this claim, a source of deep conflict is whether this 'Umaryu' is the same character as the legendary Umaru attributed to the first ever knowledge revolution. Those impatient to go after the facts have dismissed the whole thing as a passing susurrus; an old lie that has somehow survived centuries. Many others however, claim that the *Umaryu* referred to in the Book of Thoth is the 2BC individual Umaru. Other 21st AD century scholars write that *The Umaru* was one of *The Umari* code of ethics, the ultimate text, the law and scripture of the BC people. This is apparently why many late BC literatures commonly associate with or quote 'the Umaru'- a declaration of association with the authoritative text. It is still not clear why Umaru was perceived as nonconformist and what his responsibilities were either as a noble or as the ordinary man. Not much is written on the authority against which he was constantly rebelling either.

As diverse as the literature is on various aspects of Umaru, a convenient convergence of conspiracies exists in these texts. A subtle point of unanimity in diverse Umaru theories is what the word Umaru meant, what the Umaru spirit inspired, what the Umaru title represented and whether rich or poor, charitable or unkind, what Umaru the man stood for. On the meaning of the word, different texts use different descriptions but all point to a common notion; a wholesome, unending entity. Some literatures suggest that Umaru literally means perpetual. Some early BC scripts have used the words 'umaru' and 'together forever' synonymously on many instances. Others describe o'maru as representing completeness or wholeness. Translations of some 3 AD manuscripts were found to have used the word 'Umaru' to mean 'there is, there was', some form of endlessness. It is still not known why most written accounts on Umaru conveniently concur on some aspects and differ so much on all other facets. The two surviving texts thought to have been authored by Umaru were found in two places. One was found in an old tomb in the Tsodilo hills near the Kalahari of Africa and the other in the Library of Ashurbanipal in Nineveh. Although these were found distances apart, the two texts were verified by a team of prominent BC literature scholars from Cambridge, Oxford and Harvard universities. The texts were apparently identifiable by the unique signature they both had on the same spot, at the bottom left part of the scroll. This signature was a simple circular shape, followed by a scribble of what is believed to read 'there is-there was'.

O- *there is, there was*

20. Upping Ante

The piece of *Upping Ante* is a little scattered in structure but is largely about pulling up one's knickers whenever one has to. The piece directly refers to and quotes an influential scientist Louis Pasteur, notable conscious creatives Talib Kweli, Nas Jones, Tupac Amaru and Bob Marley. *Upping Ante* promotes ever readiness to seize a chance, to rise to an occasion, to pounce on opportunity, to step up. *Upping Ante* attempts to capture the interwoven brevity and delicacy of the opportunity. In one part, the piece describes 'a narrow window of opportunity to transmit one's morse'. In relation to exploiting the small opportunities, *Upping Ante* advises that in spite of the jiffy nature of a moment, something worthwhile must be accommodated somehow. This according to *Upping Ante* is because in the event that one's revolution is not broadcast, it must still be available otherwise. So when the opportunity to create or advance or transmit avails even transitorily, one must be ready because chance favours the ready.

Upping Ante

Stepping up has to be what every opportunity seeker is about. You too, have to be about stepping up. At any time, one must be the kind of character that is up to the task, whatever the task. Every time opportunity abounds, however slim, however slight and however tight the circumstance, one must be up to the task, however difficult. One has to constantly self-assure that they are up to the task, however much task may demand of one. One has been found wanting before, and missed a chance of a lifetime. One forgets not the lesson learnt from this occasion; the *found wanting* occasion is a reminder to maintain the struggle of one's cause. In one's wild readings, one chanced upon a text about Louis Pasteur who had advised that chance favours the ready. Others claim that his exact words were that chance favours the prepared mind. Either perspective is relevant to the idea of upping ante; putting in a little more if merited and whenever required.

The *ambitionist* is always after some kind of opportunity and rarely knows when this opportunity appears. It makes sense for the *ambitionist* to be ready at *all-a-times*, lest opportunity finds the *ambitionist* wanting. It is better to be prepared than to be found in the compromising position of wanting. It is no news that some prefer to wait for luck. Some a chancer lies in wait for luck and usually does *fock-all* while they wait. A religious teacher had once advised that if one was not doing what they liked, they would ultimately have to like what they had to do. Worse still they may have to do what they do not like. Upon hearing and learning of this concept one decided to like what they had to do. One advises that you too need to start doing what you like. One has made a decision in this matter and has been working at it since. At the time, one understood that to do what one does well, one has to like it. To maintain both the liking and doing, one had to learn to adapt to both the enabling environments and the not conducive ones. The environments in question refer to the conditions progressively exploited to undertake whatever it is one consistently occupies their time with. Whenever these environments seem unsupportive and hostile, upping the ante is called for.

Oftentimes, a little more vigour is demanded from one by the situation. There are certainly such times in most people's lives; when a job at hand demands a little more than the usual energy; times when the typical effort is just not enough. These are times when one has to up the ante and push a little more strongly; run an extra mile and endure a moment longer. Even when one has a full plate, finishing up is a must, getting the job done is mandatory. When you find yourself upping ante on the regular, be proud but watch out for burnout. Do not be keen to be victim to this *un-phenomenal* episode. Instead, let your aversion to burnout be what coerces you into the eternal consciousness of the intensity of your labours. This labour intensity and the urge to maintain it should not interfere with rest. Every once in a while rest is absolutely necessary. So do ye catch a breather so ye be rested not from *yown* causes but from *yown* labours. Rest so you be ready to commit a supercharged session of labour when absolutely necessary. Upping the ante when it matters -matters more than at any other time.

For one's troubles, one seeks comfort. For one's pains, one seeks relief. For one's pleasure, one bumps to underground tunes. In one's tries to advance, one has navigated treacherous waters like Talib; mentally, one maintains a purple state of mind like Nasir and is cautious of slippery slopes like Bob-Nesta. Sometimes like Amaru, one never sleeps; such are times when ante must be upped. In times like these, one is ready, prepared and in a purple state of mind, one is better positioned to navigate treacherous, slippery slopes. Discipline, the kind observed by armies of ants, is a critical part of one's attitude in such times. Will and purpose are the other pillars of the attitude of upping ante. The will to get it done, whatever it is, thrives if hinged on purpose. Maintaining focus on one's purpose enables discipline. Being in good discipline is being ready, being ready is being favourable to chance. Chance favours the ready.

21. Personal Truths

Personal truths is a personal train of thought that found its way into the text of Abstraxion. The piece is a third level retelling of my thoughts. I describe it as a third level retelling because in the piece, I write about rethinking some of my thoughts. Thinking about what I regularly think about is a mental exercise I habitually do but have never captured on paper before. In this piece, I describe my thoughts on my past mental wanders. The sophistication of my mental wanders has since become elaborate. But this is what my thoughts were like back then.

Personal truths

Occasionally, I take a few moments to self-query. The key item in my self-inquisition is usually the *why*. I self-ask why it should be worth my while to see through an undertaking. Why it has to be done and how it contributes to my purpose. Over time, my cause, my why has started to matter in almost everything I do. In almost everything I do, I try to take time no matter how momentary, to determine the value of it.

The occasional questioning of oneself is habit to an effective person. Self-critique, is also so. It is highly probable that many who undertake the exercise of occasional self-criticism can stand it because it is of importance to their development. I *questions* myself on a regular basis, at least as regular as situation occasions. The questions span a variety of concepts, things about life, economics and leverage, the *sociologicals*, the *rebeligious*- and the lot; I let the mind do the wandering. Recently I wondered about love- whether she is real or not. On another occasion, I was wondering about accounts in a commercial world. I wondered what the ultimate self-enriching account looks like, whether it is the one is my own name or the one I own in someone else's name. But then, how much leverage do I get from an account that is not in my own name? I have wondered and still do. I wonder whether I will ever find the truth, I know it is a long shot. Discovering truth while I sleep is also improbable but not entirely impossible. I imagine that the little truth I have now is mostly personal, in which case it may be of little use to the ethnic mind. Perhaps my truth may benefit another mind if only the other mind identifies with the relevance of the said personal truth. On many occasions, I wonder, I get confused by some and figure some out; I self-question and self-criticise, I resolve some and make an effort to improve some.

On economics, I wonder if my scheme would sell and what currency I would prefer to get paid in. Would I prefer any currency that affords me and my kin a comfortable life? Do I even want the kind of life that successful cash schemers lead? These are my wonders on personal economics and earthly riches. Usually I am biased towards economic gain, the gain to enable my earthly comforts. I wonder if it really is scheming if I put my passions in it. I am conscious that many who start in a position of humility claim some allergy to wealth and excess; I know that many of these ultimately realise that sufficiency is never sufficient. In my humility, I too thought that enough is enough. Or is it? I usually imagine the man, the good man; in his deserved humble comfort, earned in hard toil and luck, I wonder what he thinks of the wealth and excess that lurk stubbornly in his horizon. So what, if the good man is poor? So what, if he has excess? I wonder. The good man's conviction accompanies his currency. This way he is certain and sincere in any comfort since it was afforded by pure hustle, and some luck from the powers that be. I imagine the good man is this way because he never underestimates the value of conventional currency. Being good and all, I imagine the good man never undersells the currency of his raw values and virtues, no matter how unconventional. Sometimes in my wonders I imagine this bigger power, some power that enforces right and fairness. I imagine that I'm in its good books, this bigger power. And so in my pursuits, I try to never forget to be grateful, for whatever little I have.

In my other mental wanders, I self-question and self-criticise. I imagine that self-criticism can be an effective motivator, if the criticism is objective. I find a deliberative criticism essential to life and how I want to live mine. And so when I self-critique, I am conscious; I recognise and respect but am not intimidated by competition. My self-criticism appreciates my past efforts and recommends *upping of ante* as situation dictates or as demanded by the urgency of the pursuit. In the midst of a self-critique, I realise how realistic my ambitions of a throughput augment must be for the whole exercise to be effective. I also realise how, I as the critiqued must accept the critique in order for any improvement to take place. I find that once I have accepted my own criticism on what I need to get better at; the motivation almost always automatically follows. This helps; it helps me avoid having to wallow in self-pity after a moment of self-critique. Being able to recall my past achievements works for my motivation. After a very momentary indulgence in past glory, after I extract a little self-cheer, I start to entertain the thought that it is not the end of the world. I start to think that I still have a shot. At this point, impossible is nothing. So many times, I imagine that my self-critique works for me.

On love, I am as clueless as the other guy. I am clueless about the longevity of it. I just know that it is some force. I know it is something powerful. Whether its proper name is love or god is another matter, a question for another forum. I think it is a hard thing to quantify. I think that if anyone has to qualify their acquaintance or any affinity to love, they at-least must have experienced love, given and received it. I have learnt that when it abounds, love is a beautiful thing. And when it does not, things can be nasty. I think it is worth respecting, worth nurturing and worth experiencing. How it feels and looks like, I dare not describe in definite terms. I feel unqualified to speak for the masses on such a matter. But I do have an opinion; I think that it looks and feels like nothing I had seen nor felt before I experienced it. It find it is hard to relate to anything else I had experienced before I encountered it. Religious scripture describes it as patient, kind, trustworthy, hopeful. I reckon it is a hell of thing; this love.

In the quest to find my why in each thing I do, I have found that the grand purpose is not always vivid in everyday doings. Sometimes it seems too personal, other times it is ambiguous, once in a while it is familiar. Yet for each small thing, I make certain that I spend a small time beforehand to establish a personal worth; the worth of the small thing to my personal purpose. The few times I have pre-established the butterfly effect of an everyday doing to my purpose, I have seen it through very diligently, no matter how mundane it seemed. I don't think it's rare, to see big things in small things.

22. Commercial

One of the effects of our globalised, connected and information-driven world is concept promotion for commercial purposes. Marketing is an industry that exploded with the information boom. Today, marketing continues to exploit the connected and information driven consumerist world. The piece of *Commercial* maps the general contours of product promotion. The piece *calligraphs* the product promotion template crafted to appeal to a consumer who is vulnerable to psychological cues of persuasion. However one views product promotion, a few can argue with the accuracy of the slightly contorted scenery of *Commercial*.

Commercial

The objective, promotion of the brand; a grand campaign to revive customer awareness of the brand. The motive, to remind consumers of how ahead of the game the brand has always been.

The brand is 'best of rest', the best of the rest. Its' product is relevant to the needs of the masses. Its' use is as everyday as a household product. The brand is useful. The average person needs the brand's product. Take paid Actor A for example. He is not who he claims to be. The same applies to popular lingerie Model D. In real life, she is a well-travelled and successful professional. In the advertisement, these two are the average users of the product. In the advertisement, they demonstrate how convenient it is to have the product. In a series of primetime media advertisements, the two show how easy it is to use the product. In 20 seconds, they are done, the brand has worked. It has outperformed and outdone another unnamed, evidently obscure and less sophisticated brand. After a 20 second advert, the brand has convinced the ambivalent buyer. The undecided is sold to the brand.

A new version of the brand's product is being launched. Brand product V3.0 is the chic version of the previous model. The new product V3.0 features the latest technological advances. The use and handling of the new V3.0 exceeds the recommended International Use and Handling standards for products such as the V3.0. Giant billboards at busy airports and mega malls announce the superior abilities of the new V3.0 Product. Urban radio stations market the V3.0 with jazzy jingles and catchy phrases. Social networks are buzzing with excitement for the new product.

Politicians and celebrities have weighed into the frenzy. The President of Nowheria is said to have used state funds to order a piece of the V3.0 for each of his family members. The cabinet of the Enstranged Republic of Lestrania is reported to have approved a bulk order of ten thousand pieces for every *Lestranian*. A recent survey by the Commercial 500 publication reports that as many as 99.9% of the 500 Commercial 500 CEO's have acknowledged using the V3.0 product at least once a day. A study by the U-Not has revealed that 90% of respondents in least developed countries have rated the product as their most basic need ahead of shelter, water and food. The latest, most watched *You-Tools* video is the footage of a two year old singing the product V3.0 jingle. In the video, the young kid is dressed like the celebrity who does the advertisement on print and electronic media. At the end of the skit, the youngster stares into the camera and growls 'The new product V3.0 by the brand; Best of rest!'

The brand pays. The brand is profitable. The world's favourite sports team is sponsored by the brand. The highest paid sportsmen are the brand's ambassadors and have the brand's logo on all of their clothes. The brand is popular. Sales of counterfeit goods with the brand name and logo have more than doubled in the two weeks since the V3.0 was launched. The chairman of the brand corporation has since assured shareholders; all two of them that the fakes have not affected target sales. Market analysts were predicting triple platinum sales within a week. Apparently 'selling like hot cakes' is an understatement for the sales of the V3.0. Stock traders around the world have watched with awe as the brand stocks shot up and kept climbing. There were rumours of an impending peak but it has not happened yet. The financial press have labelled the product V3.0 a phenomenal commodity. Apparently, no product has ever sold this much and this fast since the commercialisation of salt. A *Saltology* professor at a prominent university has confirmed that the product V3.0 has decidedly surpassed the excitement witnessed during the *Saltarean* era. Apparently, the *salarium* generated from the salt trade at the time is incomparable to the profits of any other trade of that era. Salt achieved worldwide use within three years of its discovery and commercialisation. In contrast, the V3.0 was used in every household around the world in just two weeks of launch.

Check your local guides for the V3.0 specials. The product V3.0 by Brand could be at a store near you. Do not miss the opportunity to be the proud owner of a new V3.0 version of the brand's new product. The V3.0 features superior, faster and more precise functions than the previous version. Endorsements by various international stockists and retailers of the V3.0 have come from far and wide. Make your missus proud and be the bloke with the brand. Surprise your man with a new V3.0. Impress the girls and rock the brand. That guy you have been eyeing, imagine the look on his face when you show up with a new V3.0. Be a cool dad and embrace the brand. You are not quite the girl around town without the new V3.0. Show off to your mates in a brand new V3.0! Be a modern activist and swear by the brand. The new product V3.0 by the brand; Best of rest!

Disclaimer: This piece was brought to you through the financial assistance of the new Product V3.0 by the Brand. The Brand; Best of rest! Like the brand on Footbook. Follow product V3.0 on Wilter.

23. Shorthand

When one is in a creative zone and labouring to rapidly transform thought to idea, from head to paper, there are instances when thoughts are conceived in brief, abstractive, hardly logical but relevant and connected words. When the writer is in such a zone, the writing defaults to a *Shorthand*. In the *Shorthand*, facts are compressed, words are shortened and whole ideas contracted. Most of the pieces of Abstraxion are versions of the shorthand. The typical *Shorthand* is brief, efficient, *wordly-economic*, precise and nifty. The story of the *Shorthand* moves quickly and is written in the briefest of times. The *Shorthand* almost always directly or indirectly acknowledges the power of the moment. Conscious of the fleeting nature of the moment, the *Shorthand* must reconnect somehow. *Although he has to go, she will be back and he will reconnect.*

Shorthand

Fathom those who will.

A minute found, 20 seconds for the cause, not a bad trade. For those who balance grim reality and ambition to strive for better, any second for the cause is gold. Few seconds, ambitious undertakings, progress transacted. It is a journey, not a destination. The destination is unique, self-determined for each. This is why the process of the undertaking is a relevant determinant to the self-determined destination. If the journey is not worth it, neither is the destination. For this journey, inspiration is necessary, purpose is paramount and persistence is ingredient. So when an inspired, purposeful journey is traversed with some persistence, the destination is likely to stimulate in some way. Similarly for most a destination, if it stimulates, it must have involved a persistently traversed, purposeful and inspired trip. Where one is mentally at any point of the journey determines a significant lot.

Imperfectly efficient and economic.

Equality encourages fairness. Slightly contrary to equality, is the idea of means tested division. It is the wish of many for all people to be equal. However, a few people continue to actively maintain the status quo wherein some are more equal than others. The wishful think this is unfair and against supreme intentions of perfection. But then what is prefect? Not humans, certainly not their nature and not their inventions. The technology of the human is not perfect, most of it is hardly efficient. For every input into a human invention, be it a software system or hardware machine, a proportion of this input is wasted in the form of sound, imprecision, heat and miscalculation, rendering the said invention imperfectly efficient. Amongst his other inventions, the human formulated economics as a framework of trade. This framework has proven unfair, immoral in some contexts, unscientific and fragile. The economic framework is far from perfect. Despite the imperfection of the human, inspired texts call for perfection or some form of continuous strive towards it. 'Be ye perfect, as your father which is in heaven is perfect'- is one such call from the book of *Mattahu* in the *Biblus*. What the statement means, suggests and the extent of its cryptic orientation is another question, another discussion. The context of the *Mattahu* perfection and many others in most spiritual texts is discipline; the enduring kind. To the human, perfection seems too hard and unattainable despite the vastness and depth of the perfection he lives on; system earth. Why this perfection earth regularly fails to inspire everyone is a mystery. Despite her industry, organisation and perspective, the human continues to fall short of perfect. In the meantime, the inefficiency will do until the discovery, arrival, achievement or any other attainment of this illusive state, the state of perfect. This is the state the shorthand is after.

Daring- shorthand is nifty.

It takes a sum of words to adequately describe an object, concept or incident. However it takes no more than one word to be precise. The extensive *vocanomics* in the shorthand is reliant on the latter fact, that a single word is adequate to be precise. Precision, like perfection is difficult to tame but also restrictive if not confined to context. Precision is also easily misunderstood and misused. Notwithstanding the limitation of precision, the shorthand is confident. He takes a chance at precision, he figures he can do it. She thinks she is game for it, she gives it a go. He takes a shot, he hits the target. She is on point, she fancies a second helping. He creams it- yet again. She likes it- that she has done it again. He keeps at it. 'Till he makes it'- he says. She will keep at it. Many condemn him, not that he cares. Many more commend her. 'What a talent'- they say of him. 'What a waste'- they remark of her. As some commend her skill, some condemn his creativity. She wishes they would let her be, he has ambition to chase. No matter how dodgy or flawed, shorthand is keen. Despite his errors, he refuses to be frantic. She identifies with non-conformists, hers is the long game. He can't stop; he is obsessed. For each minute she finds, she spares a few moments for the cause. Desperate and pressed, shorthand is out of time. He has to go, she will be back, he will reconnect and she will do it again, take a chance at precision.

24. Currency of value and virtue

The answer, if it exists, and it must, must be about what matters most, why your born and your life purpose. But first there has to be a question. The Currency of value and virtue is a natural connection of the world's wisdom to religion, known philosophies, political governance, social movements, technical and financial systems. The currency of one's values and virtues is a connection of one's wisdom to one's self determined grand purpose. Full of bold assertions, the piece is about what one is prepared to trade for their life. Importantly, the piece is about being you, being authentic. Authentic is who you are; and when you are you, you are in touch, you think clearer, you know better.

Currency of value and virtue

Many philosophies have been proposed and accepted as truths of life and why living matters. For the religious, it is a believer's market. In politics too, different nations have varied governmental arrangements with varying levels of the citizens' approval and acceptance. Meanwhile the world's population expands while natural resources diminish. There are more people than have ever been and they are using faster and more than they are restoring. This chaos and other fears of the unknown future are important. But more important and central to human survival is individual purpose, why one is born and what their life purpose is. Most important of all, is what one is doing about it. In pursuit of the *grand purpose* and the actions that define it, life happens. Days come and go, tomorrows remain unknown while the *yesterdays* pile up in the past.

The worth of an individual to humanity is defined by their values and virtues. The behaviour, attitude and general wellbeing of any one person is determined by a measure of their values and virtues. Coincidentally, the significant among us possess some form of value and virtue. Similarly, those who have not realised their value and virtue are defined by their lack of it, and this usually devalues whatever it is they do. Depending on the context, some values are more valuable than others. Despite context, any value and virtue have to be worth something to the holder and the bestowed, anyone bestowed of these. On this basis, values and virtues are supposed to sell well; they are supposed to be worth something to the possessor. Values and virtues are meant to have some benefit to whomever adopts and harbours, observes and practises them. They must be ultimately useful even when they are not immediately beneficial to the individual harbouring them. They may not sell well today but values and virtues are worth it tomorrow. Understandably, the immediate profitability of values and virtues appeals better than some long term prospect. It is understandable too that personal gratification seems more relevant than *greater good*. It is a selfish world, competition and relativity dictate terms. It therefore makes sense that today's dominating ideologies, currencies, religious practices, philosophies, movements and systems may not be the wisest that humanity has access to but possibly the more convenient. This is also why the wise individual chooses to be defined and judged by their values and virtues.

And happiness, what about it? Who is the happy man, the happy woman? Is it the virtuous or the agnostic? Is it the conscious or the carefree? Is it the wise or the ignorant? A common saying suggests that ignorance is bliss. Another thinker cautioned that if a man has not discovered anything, he will die for he is not fit to live. One wonders what would make one happier, one's discovery of something, anything; or the bliss of ignorance. It is difficult just to imagine anyone revelling on ignorance. But how does one know they know? What good is knowledge if one cannot apply it? What is the value of perception if one cannot perceive the bigger picture? How cool is being smart if one is not wise? To be happy, one must be in sync with the moment, one must only see oneself through a self-defined perspective. One must know one's worth, one's values and virtues. One may not know all and never will but one must know that accepting that ignorance is bliss is itself ignorant. And if one must know one thing, it must be that life without discovery is death *lifelike*. So one proposes, on the question of happiness that the happy man spends his life in discovery; the happy woman does too, she is aware of her values and virtues. The happy man does too.

In terms of values and virtues that sell better today, it is a buyer's market. This market is vast, with a vast range of value and virtue in exchange. The market is a conniving jungle, one is often compelled to sneak and snake, to tangle and ambush. One is obliged by circumstance, forced by situation and coerced by environment. The vast market of present day values and virtues can also be compassionate, when true value is legal tender and when good thrives. In the vast market, the genuine sells alongside the counterfeit. One must constantly keep an open eye on what the current environment is trending, if one does not have to, one needs not join a queue. One must learn the skill and be expert. When the slightest chance comes, one must instantly pounce and make a killing. If the market is honest, one must stock the authentic; if the market is conniving, one must sell their plot. Whatever market it is, one's life must have meaning. One's values and virtues must not be worth nothing.

Many wonder why the world can't just be good. It can, it is; it is also just not fair. Many good people wonder why the world is bad. It isn't, it just has unfair people. For those who wonder who the good people are, they are the ordinary folk who decide to do good and remember to try to be good. Bad people are good folk too. They are good people who are also ordinary but decide to do bad. Some wonder if being good is virtuous, others wonder if being bad has any value. Since all people are naturally good and since all inherently have the element of bad; authenticity is closer to both value and virtue than bad and less burdensome than good. Good is unsustainable and bad is undesirable but authentic is ideal if one can stand it. Authentic is original, it is who one is, who you are. Authentic is not exclusively commercially motivated and not needlessly competitive. Authentic is the true self, ever selfish for a selfless cause. When one is their *trueself*, they are in touch with the natural mystique; they think clearer, they know better. Only when one is authentic will they know what matters most. And it matters that one knows what matters because only then will they get their *grand purpose*. When grand purpose dictates one's behaviour, attitude, work and life ethic, then one has more value and virtue than can ever be hoped for. In the meantime, the journey of discovery unfolds. One's values and virtues may not be immediately profitable but one must continually ensure that their greater good thrives, that their bad element is controlled and that the trueself is actuated. For each day spent in this state, one's values and virtues compound steadily.

25. The Ex-pression

Initially, the aim of *The Ex-pression* was to simply compile homophonic words. I decided to ensure these rhyming words are not just words but express some insight. *The Ex-pression* is based on a series of factual incidents and situations. All of the expressions of *The Ex-pression* are factual. The piece is desperate, given the demands of the chosen poetic presentation. The character of *The Ex-pression* is a certain excommunicated and exiled x-generation. The piece declares that although he is exerted by need and circumstance, his endeavour is to exceed self-expectation. As for his thoughts, they are extensive and exceptional.

The Ex-Pression

With words precise and explicit,
with eloquence to exonerate the suspect peasant.
With the conviction to exorcise wicked thought,
immeasurable fervour, persistence without expanse.
Such is the resolve of laboured, inspired expectation.
And the resultant thought, remnant from expurgation,
expedited riddance of negative mindset;
this resultant thought, exhumed from seemingly
expiring zeal,
is for some reason, nowhere near depletion.
Extracted from ever-existent ardour, it may be well be
inexhaustible;

Experimenting with expressing insight explicitly can
be excruciating.
And when the existentialist position is expedited from
raw thought to paper,
then it matters not, neither should it exasperate the
undertaker,
not when it exemplifies noble undertakings.
Inspiration extracted, thought compressed and
expressed;
experience genius, exclaim at awe, behold exception.

Excommunicated voluntarily, exists away from clan.
Exiled, also self-imposed.
Exerted, by need and circumstance.
Critic of the *que sera;* fanatic existentialist.
Excellence in all exercises, this is what the cause
expects.
Exceeding self-expectation, the endeavour always.
Exceptionally controlled discipline, never indulgent
excess.
Exploiting opportunity, even if it's just for expression.

Sapien, male and X-generation taxonomically.
Otherwise conclusively excelsior.
The nature of his thought, extensive.
Excerpts of his pieces, exceptional;
The *Ex-pression* is a good example.
Exceptionable if he has to be, attentive to constructive critique.
If not first then second- the exacta is his bet.
Patient usually, hopeful most days and occasionally expectant.
Exercise, a necessity for this extraordinary existence.
Unexpected fatality and premature extinction, his biggest dread.
So for a cough or sneeze, his expectorant relieves.

Excitable, he is exquisite.
Rapidly expedient when he has to be real and for real.
His core curriculum, to express insight.
One word to describe his writings; extemporaneous.
Exaggeration is never his objective.
Neither is it to extenuate.
Exactness is the precision,
the precision he attaches to explanations.
The explanations without which,
frustration is exacerbated.
And when frustrated, many exclaim in anger,
damning his execution of expressions.

Experimenting with expressing insight explicitly can be excruciating.
And when the existentialist position is expedited from raw thought to paper,
then it matters not, neither should it exasperate the undertaker,
not when it all exemplifies noble undertakings.
Inspiration extracted, thought compressed and

expressed;
experience genius, exclaim at awe, behold exception.

Apologies to the exasperated.
This expository, was a laboured attempt,
to extract several *homosonic* terms,
turn them into exalted expressions,
exacerbate frustrations,
exasperate the simple minded,
and mostly express some insight.
With inspiration extracted, thought compressed and
expressed;
experience genius, exclaim at awe, behold exception.

26. Woman

This piece was inspired by Nina Simone's *Four Women*. *Woman* describes the story of *Miss Digital*; a modern chick trying to find a partner online. It is the story of *Mokhadi*, the eldest daughter in a single mother-led family of eight children. Her mother *Esther*, was a woman determined to make it through a treacherous life. *Woman* tells the story of a former pretty girl who had lost her shine enduring an abusive marriage. *Woman* salutes the woman partner, shattering glass ceilings and representing the potential, ability and talent of women. The story of Woman is the story of *Nkazi*; a woman understanding that despite everything, she is a woman for a purpose and persisting with purpose, her own purpose. *Woman* is a piece for *Marbie*, for *Mokhadi*, for *Nkazi*, for *Miss Digital* and her heroine *Whitney*. It is the story of *Esther*; a woman, an extraordinary woman.

Woman

She was born at a time when men came in two colours,
bad and good. Her father was a good man, most of the
time. He was unlike her cousin's father, her dad's
brother, her uncle. Uncle Skolo did not subscribe to
any of the colours of men at the time. He had a sneaky
shade of grey to him. Being grey, he was both black
and white, good and bad at the same time. This story is
about his niece, not his grey self, nor the good self of
his brother, his niece's father. This is the story of his
niece, a sister, a daughter, a wife, a woman.

Girl Good Looking

Privately schooled, spoilt and made to believe all she
had to do was wish away and her misguided parents
would materialise it. Made to believe that all she had
to do was call it and it would rain. Little did she know
that her parents had their own childhood issues, the
kind that united them in purpose; her mum and dad
had issues that made them compatible in a
conventional marriage. The two parents overindulged
their daughter to unconsciously justify their
annoyance and lack of control of the vices they had
each developed in their childhoods. By the moral
standards of the time, she was raised well. Most of her
peers had the same undisciplined upbringing. Her
common vocabulary included phrases like greed is
good, consume everything and work is for workers.
She was not a worker; she was raised to think so.
According to her parents, there was nothing wrong
with her attitude. Her lack of common courtesy and
manners were not anybody's problem, apparently. Her
habit of indulgence was not an issue, as long as it was
nurtured by her parents. In their parental wisdom,
they ignored and somehow forgot to discourage

detrimental behaviours on their daughter. Being careless gamblers, they did not bet on their daughter's indulgent tendency maturing into laziness, despite their encouraging the conditions of such an eventuality. She grew up spoilt, became a pretty but spoilt and lazy woman. Some still wonder how she met her backward husband, some wonder if it could be that they were both psycho. He claimed some sophistication, a revolution which somehow failed to transform his attitude. Loudmouthed, he thought only after speaking. He was uncouth, lacked integrity and was disrespectful. He had no respect for his wife and for his own self. His treatment of her was undeserved, she did not deserve such *bustardry*. Over time her good looks got buried under her bitterness. She lost shine and she knew it too. In her own words, he was just a bad man, just a bad man. Why she endured just a bad man can probably only be explained by women, and so she endured him, sadly.

Nkazi Wangu

Born *pre-poverty-levels* into a third world, a while back when poverty could not be measured and being poor was a bitter bitch. She had never met her father, she knew she probably may have but she just did not know who he was. Her mother was a single parent to their family of six. She was the first of four girls and two boys. They rented a two room shack, it was large enough to shelter all of them but was barely comfortable and hardly convenient. Everything else was tough. To describe their entire situation in three words: things were hard. Her mother, the supposed breadwinner and sole family provider was self-employed in a scarcely profitable enterprise. To support the family, Nkazi's mother brewed sorghum grain into gin, a very toxic blend that bleached the local clientele's lips over time. The loyal patrons, most of whom were unemployed and undiagnosed alcoholics, were aware that the stuff was a little too strong for their unfit bodies. Despite this, they drank the homemade gin medicinally on a regular basis. Being the oldest of her siblings, Nkazi had to assist her mother sell the brew. As the oldest child, she received very little motherly attention from her *shebeen-queen* mother who herself usually had plenty of attention from her mostly outcast customers. Selling a cheap product in good demand, attention was a given. When her mother was not selling the brew, she was either making it, sourcing the ingredients for it or looking after her younger siblings. For most of her childhood, Nkazi knew better than to yearn for any attention from her mother. By a young age of eight, she had realised how poor they were, she thought that like her single mother- she too could get some desperately needed love and attention from one of the patrons who frequented their spot. Her circumstance consumed her into her mother's trade where she helped to serve the hooch. She sold her first pint of the sting, as the brew was called, at age 11. This was an incident neither her mother nor her patrons found strange or unfortunate. Naturally gifted, Nkazi excelled at customer service, drew more hideous characters to her mother's joint and the small profits trickled in. Soon she grew comfortable with her customers, she accepted that the little attention she was getting from the broke drunks was better than no attention at all. At month end, when a few of her working clients got paid, the place would swarm with thirsty revellers looking to get smashed. At these times even the unemployed usually had just enough to pay off their outstanding credit, get new credit and drown their sorry selves into silliness. It was in these silly moments that Nkazi would get attention from the lot. This happened every time the whole shebeen was grogged off. She remembers may times when she and her siblings would be the only sane souls in a crowd of mad drunks. Most of these times, Nkazi's mother would also be just a bit *crunk*, having helped herself to a couple of sips to check the toxicity of her product. When the place got busy, Nkazi would step in as the main waitress and her mum would assume a supporting role. She would also keep an eye on the little box they hid their peanut proceeds in while also entertaining the children. For all her childhood, this was Nkazi's world. It was the world of her siblings' childhood. She survived it and made it to adulthood. By age 20, she had a couple of children of her own, each by a different man, and none of whom stuck around nor bothered to help with the children's upbringing. It was a mammoth, overwhelming task. Each morning while she readied for a busy day of serving cheap alcohol, and each night after a long day, she would reassure herself that she would not fail at parenting. She struggled and persisted for her children; she had to. She was Nkazi for a reason, a woman for a purpose. Despite her otherwise doomed childhood, she swore her own children would not be doomed. This was her purpose.

Woman Partner

Corporate firm Partner at just 25 years of age, she was the youngest ever partner at Dicks and Crooks. Dicks and Crooks was a reputable law firm and established enterprise co-founded by her grandfather Bignell Dicks some 30 years back. Together with his fellow founding partner, Ben Crooks, they were known as shrewd in both law and business. *'Big Dicks'* as the old-city folk knew him was known as a no-nonsense, straight talking and hardworking man. He was her grandfather. Those who knew his father, Kenneth Dicks claim that he had the same character as his son, Bignell. Whatever character Big Dicks had, or wherever he had learnt it from, it was apparent that he was keen to maintain the legacy he and his father had established. In his days, he was known all over the city and the surrounding towns. He was a strict father too, according to popular rumour. Many use the example of Marbie, Bignell and his wife Celeste's only daughter as a perfect example of a disciplined upbringing. Nobody knew what it was precisely but there was just something about Marble 'Marbie' Beckett. She was elegant, in the way she spoke, in the way she would smile but speak firmly; her style and taste had some peculiarity to them. Like her father Bignell, she commanded respect. Marbie had herself been an attorney like her father; she had worked in the family business and had legal teams that won several landmark cases. She had turned down the firm partnership in order to care fulltime for her children. She was married to Brendan Beckett, and the two were the parents to this young woman who had just been promoted to partner at the youngest age in the firm's history. She loved the law, this young woman. She loved her career and was not afraid of the challenges. She was remarkably bright, had a head-full of ideas and was keenly interested in the justice system; its reaches, its limitations, its fairness, its effectiveness to the man it was made for, and also whether it was made for man, or man for it. At the annual Dicks and Crooks ball, it was none other than her mother, the respectable Esquire Marbie Beckett who was set to give opening remarks and announce the latest Dicks and Crooks partner. She summarised the program for the night, introduced dignitaries and paused for a short while, sighed audibly into the lectern microphone and declared "Now, it is an honour to introduce Dicks and Crooks' latest partner, the first woman partner in the history of Dicks and Crooks, the youngest ever partner in the history of this firm. Ladies and gentlemen, please join me in congratulating... " The crowd knew who it was, by the time she mentioned her name the applause had drowned out the PA system. A standing ovation ensued for a good two minutes. The glass ceiling had been shuttered once more.

Miss Digital

Miss Digi was a typical mid-21st century chick. Her way of dressing seemed like a silent protest, except it was loud, and she, she seemed switched on, she was techno; electronic through and through. She was into anything and everything digital. Technology was all she knew, not because she wanted to but because she needed to. All she knew was technological. All her files were in the cloud, she was a fan of music and always accessed her music over the net. Most of the time, she had earphones on full blast. Listening to a thumping techno riff while simultaneously browsing the net on one of her several mobile and wearable devices was an established habit. The internet was her world, and had been since she was but a babe. Most things she knew about life were learnt through the internet, directly and indirectly. Socially, she was the typical teenager; misguidedly brave, impatient at times, keen to learn and interested in love, *Fashion and Cool*. She, like many her age, hoped to fall in love someday. She had always maintained her preference to falling in love rather growing into love. She claimed she did not fully understand the difference between the two but the little she knew about love convinced her that she would rather fall into it. She had never met any of her

1508 friends and had only interacted with them virtually; yet 327 of them were in her virtual close circle. To find a soulmate, Miss Digi employed the services of two online dating sites. This was her best shot at finding the most compatible partner. She completed a questionnaire which was a prerequisite parameter to the algorithm that computes a compatible partner from a pool of male and female candidates. She deliberately decided not to specify the gender of her potential partner. Once she hits find, the system does its heuristics and ranks the top five candidates in order of suitability and irrespective of gender. It was therefore possible that these top candidates could be a mix of men and women or all be of the same gender as the seeker. This was the point for miss Digi, she trusted the system. She and thousands of other subscripts of the site found this N-S-A-A, not strange at all. A lot many self-professed staunch heterosexual users of the site had been recommended partners of the same gender, sometimes even after specifying the opposite gender as a preference. The system knew better. In her case, three of Miss Digital's top five candidates had caught her eye. She just needed time to analyse the metadata of the two attractive girls and the guy she thought was the most interesting of the two men in her top five list. She knew that all three of them fitted her specification for a perfect partner. However, she wondered which of them would comply with her most important requirement. Although the pictures they posted in online social forums suggested that they lead functional and normal lives. Their mostly ignorant and rarely consistent posts showed they were fairly human. Still, she wondered just how many of them would pass her most vital requirement, the reality test. In her experience with other similar sites, there was a good chance that none of her top three were real persons. 'Oh-What the hell'- she whispered as she clicked on the profile of her first candidate. She had momentarily paused the music in her mobile device to remind herself of *chardi-kala*, that all was well. She hit play, the chorus resumed: 'I, I, I, I'm every woman', she was grooving to a house remix of the Whitney hit.

Esther

Then there was Esther. Born into hardship, she avoided talking about her childhood. When she did, she only told happy stories. She never told any sad ones, except one where her sister got gored by a tree brunch which exposed her intestines. How well she remembers the other sad stories in her past was hard to guess. To her children, she was the biggest example of forgiveness they knew of. She must have been born a mother because it seemed it is all she had ever been. Her little known and largely hidden history did not seem as happy as the stories she usually told. She was born into male domination and raised by a poor, unmarried woman in a patriarchal society. It was a men's world she grew up in. She in-turn, became a single mother of eight and was never married. This was unsurprising given her seemingly inspired stubbornness. She lived the events and endured the unfair conditions of her childhood. Singlehandedly, she raised her family with determination and hardwork. She made it a point to be there for her children, their children and their children. The wisdom and experience she had accumulated over the years was undoubtable. She was also human, and had her share of errors. Being strict, she tolerated very little childishness from her children. She is known to have occasionally uttered a few swear words, usually in the heat of the moment when one of her children was trying to be impossible. One of these children was Mokhadi- her eldest daughter. Mokhadi knew her mother more than anybody else. She took her oldest sibling role seriously. Like her mother she was determined. She decided one day that one of the things she would do to honour her mother was write a piece on women, an abstract on their struggles, joys, pains and passions. When opportunity arose, Mokhadi put pen to paper and scribbled the story of Woman. In the opening line, she describes a woman born at a time when men came in two colours, bad and good.

27. Catchyoucatchinacold

Catchyoucatchinacold is not a holier-than-thou piece but instructs the fellowmen to stop making excuses. Finger-pointing and blaming others for *self-faults* are the two behaviours discouraged in the piece. The agenda of *Catchyoucatchinacold* is that each time you rest, another plods away. While no moving sermon is intended by this piece, its' message is simple; do take responsibility and don't get caught catching a cold.

Catchyoucatchinacold

Many self-respecting selves will not want to be associated with finger pointing and *excusating*. The same selves will acknowledge that failure to accept and take responsibility for self-flaws is not sustainable to self-respect. *Excusating*, habitually making excuses for oneself will not coexist with self-respect. Similarly, just accepting one's flaws and not taking the requisite corrective steps is like rotating through a fixed pivot, though there is movement, there is no resultant displacement after a full *revolvement*. The same is the case when the fault is recognized but nothing is done about it because it is no fault of one's. When the fault occurs once more and several times more and each time it is still no fault of one's, then this is excusating, and this is how one gets caught catching a cold.

In some scheme of something, cold is below hot. Above all, it is not hot. Cold can be extreme, to the extent of freezing. Cold is ideal for some. For some, cold stifles movement and encourages idle stillness. Stillness has its merits and this is how cold benefits some. For some, stillness can only be beneficial if *precursed* by a sustained measure of *unstillness*. The stillness should be brief and not as sustained as the preceding and shortly following *unstillness*. Only then can a dose of stillness be of merit and only then can cold be ideal. In other cases, cold sends shivers down spines and overwhelms transformation. When one is cold, one is slow, slack, sluggish, slothful. *When your cold, your inactive*, immobile, innately inert. When you are cold you are not creative, when you are not creative you are not productive and when you are not productive you are not living. What good is your life if you are not living? What is the worth of existence with no *livity*? Livity is lively, always moving and rarely still. Livity knows stillness sustained equals catching a cold.

In the heat of *tings,* cold sits on the extreme opposite of hot. The alternative to cold, hot is not still. If anything, hot undoes stillness. Without some hot, the cold blooded creeper is motionless, exposed and vulnerable. Energetic and rearing to go, hot is restless for cause. Doing is what you do to stay hot because doing creates heat and melts the freeze. Hot can be as detrimental as cold. At its extreme, hot is not so ideal. In some situations, hot is destructive and contorts original form. In these situations, hot debilitates core function. To avoid burnout, hot requires constant moderation and the occasional small measure of cold. This way, unstillness is sustained through regular resets of brief stillness. When sustained accordingly, hot and cold coexist. But when hot is uncontrolled, one burns out and may catch a permanent cold shortly after.

In other schemes of other things, it is neither hot nor cold that is ideal. The ideal state in these schemes is warm. Warm is *arite*, not hot and not cold, just arite. Even for these schemes, it is worse still to be caught catching a cold. Catching a cold is when one is inactive for more than is necessary. Inactivity is dormancy; only seeds find dormancy beneficial. Dormancy is hibernation and hibernation is for some animals. Even they do the necessary to ensure that the dormancy is brief and followed by sustained wakefulness. Don't be dormant, don't be cold, not for too long. Don't catch yourself catching a cold. Don't let anyone catch-you-catchin-a-cold.

Catchyoucatchinacold..*v2*

So, whatever one may do,
however one may spend,
the moments of their short life,
one must not just understand,
not just constantly remind themselves,
and not just be perpetually conscious,
that time is running out.
Instead one must be one with time.
One must never be out of sync with time.
Because when they do,
then one is catching a cold.

The scenery of *Transitory* is only exemplary,
to not just the beauty of nature,
the poetry of thriving,
and the power of hustle.
It is also an inspiration,
this scenery, space and state
that bore the thought of *Transitory*.
So one must never be found wanting.
Not in inspiration.
Because when this happens,
then one is catching a cold.

Eyes open, ears attentive,
mind alert, all day and every day,
of one's short life.
So the way one sees it,
the way one perceives it,
and the way one abstracts it,
reflects this sensitivity,
to one's seen, felt and heard surrounding.
If one loses this sensitivity,
then one's abstractions are compromised.
When one can't abstract,

then one has caught a cold.

Must not procrastinate, one will not delay.
One can never have an excuse,
Excusating is a common tendency.
Finger pointers swear by it,
but *purpose-chasers* hate it.
So excuse must fall.
Because when one is excusating,
one is catching a cold.

Envy, revenge, hatred.
Out of time, wanting inspiration.
One must be free of these and other burdens.
One must be light to oneself,
to carry and move oneself with efficiency.
Sedulous with value,
one must not to be indebted.
One must awe all but owe no one.
When one owes another,
then one is catching a cold.

Pay your dues,
do the needful,
and don't get caught.
Don't catch yourself idle.
Don't catch yourself purposeless.
Don't catch yourself,
catching a cold.

28. Transitory

One cold winter day on the 640 morning train from Ballarat Victoria to the Southern Cross station in Melbourne Australia, a man on his way to work, sat next to an elderly woman who had her earphones on and was listening to something seemingly engaging. The man opened his work bag and removed a notepad and a couple of pens. He pulled back the retractable tray attached to the seat before him, set his notepad on the tray-top, held one pen between his right hand fingers, shut his eyelids momentarily and started writing in a hurried manner. He was aware of the elderly woman next to him, who was not so engaged anymore to whatever was playing on her handheld digital gadget. The man was also feeling the strange stares of those around him. Within a few minutes, many who were on nearby seats had taken a leisurely but noticeable interest to the man's writing. Despite it all, he continued writing. *Transitory* was the title of his piece that day. In the first line, he argues that without movement, life is somewhat compromised. The piece of *Transitory* celebrates creativity and the utilisation of creativity irrespective of circumstance, state or setting. The writing of *Transitory* took place when one was awake to the negative pressures and in a state to stare down opposing attitudes in order to progress one's cause.

Transitory- Reflection in motion

Without some movement, some form of transition, some form of change, the idea of life is compromised. Herein, a *reflectory* note, a transitory thought borne in physical transition.

Pressure felt, inspiration unleashed, performance delivered. This is who he is in his own definition, formidable and inspired. No wonder it came with such ease, even though it did not. Had to be pressed off somehow, this inspiration. Milled in thought, rich in jnana, stemmed in relevance, laden in perspective, nothing definitive, not a thing absolute. This way, albeit peculiar, it enriches and defines personality; a specific connection with a particular way, a particular being. When pressure becomes the very catalyst to inspired delivery, his attitude is to face it head on, for what it's worth.

For the opportunities chanced upon and exploited; this is still his philosophy. This is what the school of small chances reminds and what the church of little moments teaches. The notion of small movement is still what he swears by. Of the small movements, thus has been said; that they are the cause of impact; incomprehensible precursors to continental tectonics. It has been said that they precede giant quakes and slides; that they are the small steps that form giant leaps. The same way that the Abstraxion is the combined wholeness of small abstracts.

When compromise approaches, when disruptive threats mock in the horizon, when the opposition is driven by envious fear; care must be taken to ensure that the ideas, the thoughts and ways of progressive transition are advanced and expressed. The burdens of the calling, no matter how self-inspired, must not be forgotten. The purpose of the movement, no matter how small, must constantly be on one's mind. The path of the cause must be perpetually treaded, no matter how distant the destination. Impossible is nothing, if these and the requisite labours are realised and pursued fervently.

The challenge of the fervent pursuit of requisite labours of personal callings are like being in a deep, dark and dense valley. The reality of the depth of these valleys must be acknowledged, as should the seemingly unbearable pressures, the common lapses of willpower and occasional questioning of one's capabilities. In dire cases, some even question the need for their own lives. When times are desperate, it is common for desperate thoughts to dominate one's mind. It is seldom easy for the character in strife to let go. Because desperate thoughts have taken over, the character in strife is unconscious to purpose, hence the disregard to whatever calling one has defined for themselves. This also explains the ease with which the character in strife's life is wished away when times are pressing. A common saying describes work being cut for the worker. The insinuation behind the phrase holds a weight of verifiable truths; all who go after worthy pursuits have their jobs cut out for them. Because these worthy pursuits are self-defined, the said truths are personal and so is their relevance. The weight of a worthy personal pursuit however, is some burden. And so, with opposing *pressury* forces assembled, inspiration acquired, transitory or stationary, the fervent pursuit of a personal calling must not cease. Any small piece is a key part of the whole. In the end it comes together and is a delight. The delight of any small achievement of the personal pursuit is a thrill, a joy to keep for life.

145

Ignoring familiarity, snubbing acquaintance, feigning some deep trance, it has to be done, the pursuit must persist. For the time being, the debt from a begrudged acquaintance is worth it; the scorn well earned from one's snub of acquaintance in pursuit of the cause is transformed and redirected into inspiration. It is the same inspiration ingredient in each scribble, each *piece-offering*, indeed in each activity fulfilling the pursuit. For him, on one particular transit; the activity of the pursuit began with a pen on paper. Before long the pen proceeded to sketch an abstract. This was preceded by a thought guided only by infinite imagination. For the moment it seems insignificant, it seems immaterial. A quick scan of it reads appears like an *abstract ramble*, a page of *doodle-scribble*. This is what is seems like initially, but this is not what it is meant to be. It is meant to be more. It is a labour, a sweat of the brow, one's love, pain and passion. This is the pursuit in a personal context. This is what his pursuit is for this transitory period.

In one transit one morning, he remembered, that this *pen-paper-pursuit* is his life, his *strive and thrive*. This is his chosen occupation, this is why he does it with purpose. Even on transition, he is on that deep thought, this time on account of the labouring proletariat, the free slave and the perpetual freedom-fighter. It is his way of giving, it is how he chooses to live, it is the quality associated to his life and the worth credited to it however quantified or rated. The pen-paper-pursuit is on point on perspective on all subjects all times. It has no role model, it is unlike anything seen or perceived otherwise before. It aspires to be like no other; none presently existent is like it. It is from the depths, delivered on peculiar touch and heartfelt. The pursuit follows no specific path. It consults widely on varied perceptions and subscribes to the view that all is personal. On his pursuit he posits that life's constant variable is such that the consequent to any happening is a pseudo-random outcome. He proposes that even though some things happen to encourage life's accidence and randomness, anyone that persists ultimately gets dealt an intended outcome. He holds it that there exists plentiful in life and that all of it is susceptible to manipulation and adaptation. Despite these vulnerabilities, he believes in the beauty of things.

After enduring deep, dark valleys and persisting through inconveniences and accidents; after pressury forces have been resisted and after opponents have retreated; after the long run when a good fight is fought and finished, when fellow connectionists are finally in sync; then the unravelling unfolds. It appears effortless and seems perfect; it is anything but. Rarely is it about the finish, the polish or lack of. Deep perceivers will discern touch in whatever form she appears in. Them too will catch a whiff of her wherever she hides. And so early in the morning, in transit; an imperfect, unpolished work of touch was created. He is the cause of it, he effected it. Irrespective of how it reads, be conscious to what it means. Understanding is barely necessary, not in this translation. Understanding has its limits; understanding is dependent on the logical capacity of its seeker. Consequently, the irrelevant application of logic has driven many illogical; away from the very thing sought. So judge it not, for you know not that the less the attention to logical convention, the more transcendent it becomes. In a brief trance, while transiting, he effected it; he laboured for self before he laboured for system.

29. Squeezed middle

Squeezed middle was the Oxford Dictionary's 2011 word of the year. The dictionary is a conventional source for a formal definition of who or what the squeezed middle is. This piece provides an alternative, informal perspective and interpretation of who and what the squeezed middle is. The idea of this interpretation is that if a certain part of an interdependent society is adequately squeezed or pressed economically, socially or some other way; the entire society ultimately bears the effects of the squeeze. This piece argues that the ultimate collapse of the system given a squeezing of the middle is guaranteed, on the basis that the middle is directly connected to the other two parts of society; the top and the bottom; the peasants and landlords. The piece asserts that the intricacy of the economic system and its integration with many variables makes it vulnerable to instability. The piece of *Squeeze middle* warns that the said vulnerability makes it difficult to argue against the predicted collapse of the system. The *Squeezed middle* is a take on what is known to be an elaborate subject of economics.

Squeezed middle

The following simplistic hypothesis is informed by observations of everyday economics and should not be mistaken for a formal lecture on modern economics. The opinion may be authoritative but it is far from mainstream. The grand proposition of this hypothesis is that the entire society ultimately feels the squeeze following any stress of the middle class. The current system is built such that any squeezing of the middle class has a direct *squeezy* effect on the other parts of society, the elite and the poor. For the system, the *squeezed middle* is ultimately the entire society, all of us. The following is a perspective on the economics and mechanics of the squeezed middle. It is not quite formal but it is not novel either and has several times been presented in different forms. The perspective is about the impending collapse of the system. This perspective is pertinent; its' truth is neither popular nor conventional but it is known. A thorough assessment of the logic, reason and the relevance of the perspective must convince that the squeezed middle is not just some select part of society but all of us.

For the system, the squeezed middle is the debt ready majority. Those whom the system estimates can be borrowed some purchase power to be repaid in hard currency with interest. In this day and age, only a few can claim non-conformance to the demands and delights of the squeezed middle. Items of comfort cost more than what the average citizen can afford at once. Items of necessity cost more than what the working man is prepared to pay at once. Statistically, the working man is the mode and the working woman is the majority. This is why the squeezed middle is most of us, almost all of us. Well, in many cases, all of us.

According to the system's calculations, the squeezed middle ranges from the average to those just over the average. This is certainly the case in many economic systems and it is the case in the global economic system. In economic circles, any man or woman's worth is determined primarily by their account balance plus investments minus good debts. What a man or woman can mathematically purchase determines their worth to the system. Over the years the system has grown intricate and integrated, mostly due to its insensitivity, greed and great appetite to convert anything tangible or otherwise into a form of credit. Compounding interest and negative credit have not helped the complication of the system. In addition to numerous complications, the system has countless sophisticated fragilities. Inflation, deflation, governing bodies in deficit are a few of these. For just these faults, why would anyone dismiss those who predict the collapse of the system?

In the current economic system, prices of some commodities determine the prices of some other commodities which determine national economies' gross domestic productions, which determine economic policies which determine inflation rates, the rates of which determine interest rates which determine estate prices which determine how much a mortgage is worth which determines how much one owes their bank which determines a man or woman's worth to the system, which determines what one can purchase. If the wage earner immediately finds relevance to this analogy, it is not by choice but because it applies to him, it describes her situation. Meanwhile the *landlordship* prospers because it is not the squeezed middle. The landlordship is he who the systems favours for the moment. Momentarily, the landlordship is neither in the middle nor squeezed nor pressed in any financial way. The moment of the landlordship will not last for long because the system is self-controlled, the few who claim to understand it do not get everything about it. This truth is hardly acknowledged by the system's purported custodians and masters. Behind closed doors, they admit that the continuous squeeze on the middle is hurting their interests; they admit that the system has grown a mind of its own. This, is why it is folly to dismiss those who predict the impending collapse of the system.

The facts and implications of climate change are the subject of a great debate in the scientific community. Climate change as an agent of global degradation is validated and supported by some scientists, only to be disproved and dismissed by others in the scientific community. The latter argue that the global climate is not changing for the worst. Numerous arguments, propositions and proofs have been cited by protagonists of climate change. Likewise, those who deny the claim of climate change offer counter arguments and cite proofs to support their disclaimer. Those who believe that anthropogenic global warming is happening have warned that the squeezed middle is paying heavily for the effects of climate change. They claim to have the data and numbers that prove that the middle class pays the most for the effects that affect the entire society. Apparently, the data shows that global warming is directly linked to greenhouse gas emissions. As they would have it, the emissions are from the developed man's machine revolution; combustion engine vehicles, heavily powered and heavily polluting plants, assembly lines and factories. They claim to have observed that these vehicles, plants and factories are mostly powered by some non-renewable earth resources. They further reason that the massive combustion of non-renewable fuels and

151

mass consumption of other global resources is leading to a global depletion. They conclude that because of the nature of the system, the already high price of the resource rises higher as its demand grows. Subsequently the ever-rising cost of living tightens the squeeze on the working class. The average man and woman can barely keep up with the expense of existing. Meanwhile as the earth's resources dwindle and climatic patterns worsen, the whispers of *melting-icelands* get louder. These are the proponents of climate change, and they warn that the warming globe is a precursors to a looming collapse.

If and when the system collapses, it will not only be the squeezed middle who bear the impact of the imploding weight. The ripples of the collapse will be far and wide reaching, the entire society will be shaken, the wealthy, the destitute and everyone else will be at its mercy. The collapse will be endemic. The Coney contagion of the 16th century may just be too bleak to compare to the system collapse but it will be depressing still. There will surely be some temporary chaos before the system resets or before a wholly new system replaces it. For the time being, only a total re-think and re-design of the system can save it from collapse. Any rethink must firstly recognize that the squeezed middle is the majority and therefore must attempt to address the plight of the majority first. The redesign must be fair to all, it must not disadvantage the middle class in any way, just as it must not deter the croesus or the impoverished in any way. The currency of one's values must be apportioned accordingly, whether one is the minority, the average, the majority, the tenant, the landlord, the mogul or the beggar. The rethink of the system must be systematic, it must avoid disorder and must discourage confrontation. It must be for all of us, for our sole benefit. All must understand this, especially those involved with the redesign. When it is done undoing the damage of the previous system, the new system must remove societal classes and restore equal access for every member of society. There must not be a single squeezed middle in the new system.

30. Khukhi

Written for my unborn child, *Khukhi* is a father's gift to his offspring; some coordinates to help Khukhi get started, some context, some history, some wisdom, some point of reference to help Khukhi establish some direction. This is a letter to kin and next of.

Khukhi

It's become important for me to take time to share some of my thoughts on things with you. Each day, I feel the urge more than I did the day before, the load gets heavier by the day. Since I found that you exist, I have been taking time to get things done. It is usually not the doing that takes longer, it is the decision to do I mull over a bit longer. I am also a little scared that I may share the wrong things, which I have plenty of. I feel that some of these wrong things may interfere with your exploitation of life, or whatever mode of interaction with life you decide to engage. I have also realised that every day I get a little desperate, I can't wait to see you but I worry that I may not be ready for you. I am aware of the many that have traversed this path and claim to have had the best time of their lives. So I too look to the challenge of my life if you are it. This is for you KhuKhi, for kin and next of.

The greatest thing I have learnt to date is to learn itself. With learning, there isn't a thing you could not do. I found that if you persist, the object you persist upon becomes more apparent with each ounce of persistence. I will not dare dictate to you or anybody else how to live your life, and this piece is not about that. Instead, these are my opinions, fallible as they may be but from the depths of my heart and only meant to enrich you somehow. I decided to share a thought with you because I feel it is worth your while to know your blood and your bloodline. We are a long line of mentalists, you and I. We are independent thinkers and have always advanced our fellows' thinking. We bring the distant idea closer to home. We get it, and we go get it for what it is worth. We are not ones to drop the ball, we keep it tight, we stay real, we stay relevant. In a simplistic world, we specialize in complexity, we don't conform, we swim *anti-tide*. You and I, we are a noble people, we may not hold conventional authority today but we rule the intellect. We count where it matters, in the mind.

Life is still a lesson in progress for me. I wish I could simplify it for your sake but I fear that if I am wrong I may not live with myself. But I might as well die now if I had no thought on the matter. So on life, I think it is a beautiful thing. The fact that you have such many years, days or hours on earth to do whatever it is you want amuses me. I tend to take the *longevitist* attitude on life, I live the now for later. I invest in my moments, I have learnt that every once in a while, moments invested into become instantly dividend when one needs to relive a past to wade through a current. So I invest in my moments for my wellbeing, for now and the next time I may need it. I plan whenever I can. My plans do not always come to light but the planning helps me maintain some level of control of my life. Sometimes things get bad, life gets a little bitchy, a little prickly. Some people choose to be victims to the pricks of life. Victims give up, they tend to be helpless and are mostly bitter and sad. Victors have no energy to waste on bickering, they certainly have no energy to waste on giving up. I too KhuKhi, have no excess might to waste on negativity. I find it is easier to go through life with fewer people to blame for various failures, I believe it's even better to have no one to blame for anything. One must take accountability for their actions. Despite this, there will be disappointment from those you trust and those you count as friends. In spite of this, you will engage your neighbour, you will learn from and teach your fellow. If there be a distraction of any kind from a friend, you will take appropriate action to ensure your own self-preservation. In case you never notice, the disappointing friend is oftentimes ensuring their own self-preservation through the disappointing act. So *sheba da-* watch out Khukhi.

Anything worth something I ever started, I made sure I finished. Any effort is worth something so put a good price on your efforts and get about to get it. When you find it that is worth pursuing, pursue it with urgency. Run after it and keep at it. Before you know it, you will have it, you will be at it and you will be it. Some pursuits will take longer, some will be harder but each is worth it, so get at it with a sense of purpose. At any point of your pursuit of whatever it is worth pursuing for you, understand that if anybody can, you can. You have it in you, you are it KhuKhi. Apparently we are what we do, but as at the moment I put down this thought, I am still not sure what I am but darn sure that I am a doer. I have done some cool things, I still do cool things and will do more cool things until I am too cool for cool things. They are only cool because they are incidental, accidental and relevant to my pursuits. And this is why I do them in the first place. I am what I do for me, for Tau, for Una, for my kin and next of.

I think thought is like seed Khukhi. Just as a seedling shoots through the surface into a small plant, the abstract crystalizes into a comprehensible idea. Just as the seed needs a little moisture, a raw thought needs a little nurture, think it through and you will figure it out. The thought I share in this piece was carefully thought for you. It is all I am to date, it is the best gift I have given you yet. I am your father, whatever is in me is in you. If anything, you are the superior species. Having gotten where I am with little, I will ensure that if you ever wanted to get a little further, then you have a little more. I wish that you make it in life; this is what loving fathers wish upon their offspring. Mostly I wish that you do what you find engaging, stimulating or whatever it is your definition of cool is. If you live to be old enough to understand this piece, you will also know that although I have not covered everything, I have also not hidden anything. Life for me has been a product of my learnings and doings. I would rather be doing these two than anything else. So naturally, I can only prescribe my own medicine. So take heed, be objective, be fair, be firm and let your nay be nay and your yay, yay. And always remember, you are it.

31. YHWH-SOS

YHWH-SOS is an intercessor's prayer. In the piece, the intercessor declares identity and association with the fellow mystified, those with little divine understanding. The intercessor claims that his prayer must represent all or else it fails its objective. The prayer appeals for understanding of the mystery that is life. The prayer presents inquisitions on who one is, how one self-identifies and self-defines. The questions attempt to unravel who one is and who one must be. The overarching confusion is on whether one should even be trying to figure out who they are, whether they matter and why life has to be a mess sometimes. *YHWH-SOS* is what one would say if one had a chance to meet the source, the ultimate.

YHWH-SOS

This, a massive undertaking of mass representation, an *intercedory* assignment on behalf of the bemused masses. As erroneous as one is on many an occassion, never without fault and ever imperfect, one has not tired in assuming mass representation on matters that matter. Addressed to the supreme, for the attention of the powers that be, in humility and acceptance of mortality; this is our prayer; to find self.

To define self, it is important that one acknowledges their inherent selfishness and accept that it is a common unifier of humanity. All living-things are selfish, not by nurture but by nature. Who one is and how one identifies themselves is also a common confusion among the living. So who is one, who is I? Yahweh declares that I am who I am but how does one define themselves? Is one a revolutionary, master hustler or the average citizen chasing common chores like his average fellow? Is one honest in their quest for a better life or is one a sick victim of poverty, twisted by his surrounding and consumed by his circumstance? What is better for one, is it to live in riches or live from day to day? And the injustices to some by others, should one be fighting these? How about the philosophies? Which of them is wiser, which of the several truly leads to longevity? Between self and identity, which of these two comes first, is it the self or the identity? Am I myself before my people or am I my people before myself? And my people, who are they? Was one born to mother earth or to *nkazi*, the everyday woman? And who does one represent in their causes? Does it matter? Does it depend on the circumstances of the representation? And one's circumstances, the unending struggles; is there an end to them?

This poverty one was born into, is there a solution to it? Is it money one needs to be free? And this money, is it the ultimate benchmark? Is it a fair and accurate measure of value? Are other means and alternatives to value worth it? Where exactly should one be investing their energies? What should one be chasing after? Should one be about getting they cream? Should one be stocking it up in offshore accounts and investing in stock and bond? Is it really a root of evils? One fears no evil and lives by the sweat of their brow. But is work the thing to live for? Should it be the thing one lives by? And one's wage for one's work, is it fair? Has it ever been just? Is it worth the trouble? Should one be working harder or playing harder? Should one be trying to figure it out? Is there some truth to it? Is there truth at all? Will the people ever know it?

One has heard that truth can only be relevant within a finite context. Apparently the proposition that truth is universal and timeless is a non-truth. Apparently truth is mortal and has a use-by date. This, apparently is not just true for truth only. It applies to most other living-things. Accordingly, all is vain and nothing is definite. Apparently the wise are foolish and the seeing are blind. How can this be? What is and what is not? Is there some formula to equate it all to some quantity, some constant perhaps? And on equality, was one created equal to all? Or is it that some are more equal? Is there a solution to the societal inequality? Is it a consequence of man's greed and insensitivity? Is it by divine command that man is impartial? Can it be changed? Can equality be an economic feature? Would there be a need for economics if this was the case?

If there was a way, however illusive, however mystical but existent still; if there was some way that one could tread to get to the source; and once one got there, had the audience of the powers that be. Once in the presence of the supreme, well after the obeisance bows and praises, exaltations and tributes and when one has been granted the opportunity to address all that is, what does one say? Who does one speak for? Is it just for oneself? Is it for the oppressed, the poor? Is it for the unhappy, the trapped? Is it for the travelled, the commercial? Does one represent the enforcers, or the enforced? If there was a way, however long, however treacherous; a way that one could follow to be in direct audience with the Alpha Omega. And once one got there, after formalities and *ritualities*, when one finally has a chance to address the supreme. What school of thought does one proclaim then? Is it the thug mansion one enquires about? Is it the second coming one expresses interest in?

What in the heavens is going on?

32. Che tempo che fa

This is a theory on the future of the future; a time when the *homo-alpha* inhabit the place of the current *sapien-sapien.* The human of the future, the *Alpharean,* will undoubtedly have the smarts and technology. Whether he will have the wisdom to make her world a better place is not obvious. The piece of *Che tempo che fa* forecasts the temperature of tomorrow, a summary of the world of the future. The discovery of life changing technology is important. But it is more important to guard against the loss of our human independence. Irrespective of the technology, spirituality and systems of tomorrow, it should otherwise be a bright future. Botox will be better and balding will be a thing of the past.

Che tempo che fa

Tomorrow, it is going to be very cold in some parts of the *alphabitat*. In other parts it will be hot, very hot. Age will be irrelevant in many contexts and very young people will be in power. Tomorrow, ability and activity will determine a good share of what is today determined by age. Young today will be old tomorrow, such will be the standards of the day. The technology of tomorrow will be *sick,* sick as in *ill.* Computing machines are about to get the gigs of their lives. Tomorrow will usher in a host of technological advances. There will also sadly be advancements in the technology of the unnecessary. Health-wise, tomorrow's humanity will see a global rise in obesity; the difference between fit and unfit will be more blurred than ever. Advanced medical workarounds will fix but not heal. Food prices will rise, the food itself will be heavily *chemicalised.* Tomorrow's global war may well be over and about food. For the first time, food security will mean food security. Life tomorrow will be more demanding than it is today. According to evolution, the human of tomorrow, the *homo-alpha,* will be several decades smarter than the current sapien sapien.

The technology of the future will be out of this world. Driven by unbelievable bandwidth and a *technoholic* consumer base, things that machines will do supposedly to improve the quality of human lives will be countless. How the post-modern man became so dependant to technology will be a sad story of the past, a subject of history in the future. Not all technological breakthroughs will be futile and detrimental to man's self-reliance and independence. But also, not all *clean energies* will be fuelled by non-renewable resources; some will probably be purely clean. Autonomous systems will run tomorrow's cities and industries. The home will also benefit from this giant leap for mankind. Fridges, TVs and hair-dryers will be connected in an *adhoc* network and equipped with some level of artificial intelligence. Cleaning, laundry, cooking and other chores will probably be stories of old. To showcase the previous generation's technology, museums of tomorrow will host exhibitions of today's latest toasters and vacuum cleaners. The dominating intelligence of tomorrow will be artificial. Humans will not need to remember or know much.

Tomorrow, the cold days will be quite cold, the warm days will not be warm enough for comfort either. Temperature fluctuations will not be a subject of speculation any more. The effects of an ageing and depleted eco-system will be visible, felt, breathed and lived. Unless man's smarts have found a fix to delay the materialization of the disintegrating, deteriorated earth. Natural disasters will still be natural, brutal and insensitive to human conveniences. Hurricanes will still wreak havoc, tornadoes will spread destruction and cyclones will continue to be a source of insurance institutions' making and unravelling. Earthquakes will have the same old picture in the media; confusion and shock; except tomorrow's picture will be much more vivid, ultra-high definition. Volcanoes, floods and bushfires may well be as common as sunny days. Despite the increasing intensity of the sun, energy prices will be at an all-time high; unless man has smartened up and figured the right balance for the technology, economics and efficiency of clean energy. Although many have today offered clean living as an alternative to the modern energy crises, its competitive edge as a practical solution to a consumerist and indulgent population is still uncertain; the practice itself is laden with unbearable inconveniences.

165

Humanity tomorrow will be a little less humane than it is in today's currency. This will be largely influenced by the changing conditions of the humans. The worsening human condition will prompt man to evolve or get extinct. Tomorrow will be worse for wildlife than it is today. Most wildlife will be completely extinct, a few will only exist as disproportionate *taxiderms*. The great-great grand generation of the modern humans will not know about and will physically encounter a lot less animals than the current generation. The few who will encounter or see living wildlife tomorrow, will mostly do so at some contained enclosure or some other manmade, inexact replica of the animals' natural habitat. There will not be any wildlife in the wilderness because there will be no wilderness tomorrow. The idea of natural habitat will have died a quiet death.

For humans, kindness and acts of it will mean very little. The scarcity of resources and amplified fragility of life will render it worthless for anybody to undertake an act of kindness unless there is a direct and immediate benefit to the undertaker. Naturally, this will lessen the kindness element of the act. The value and virtue system of tomorrow will be vastly different to today's. Time will be worth more than money. To the people of tomorrow, time will be life. Hopefully, tomorrow's generation, *generation-Alpha*, will know more about gratefulness than the current sapien. The living condition of the *homo-alpha* will be tight, quite tight. Most will not live beyond four decades. To a large extent, the condition of the homo-alpha will dictate that each *Alpharean* realises the preciousness of life and appreciates each day spent alive. Spirituality may be a mysterious matter tomorrow, a strange thing to many. The few spiritually conscious will not have a religion but will subscribe to a host of disparate philosophies from various old

166

religious movements. The infamy of man's fallibility would have rid the logical *Alphareans* of the common modern religious philosophies where some special man was born perfect and only did good. Despite their inherent vulnerability to logic, some Alphareans will acknowledge miracles and harbour attitudes of hopefulness and belief in some greater power.

Tomorrow's man's knowledgebase will primarily consist of numbers, machine readable only bytes. Most of tomorrow's man's knowledge will be held by autonomous machines rather than by the man himself. The mass transformation of ideas from paper books to electronic sources will be a precursor to a sharp decline in readership. Electronic sources will make knowledge readily accessible on demand, thereby eliminating the need to read and store knowledge in one's head. There will be a reduction in the liberal production of new ideas. The knowledge of tomorrow will lack depth, will be too specific, will only be relevant in a narrow domain and will serve only a contextual purpose. Intense competition for jobs and livelihoods will compel many to only learn what they need to be paid.

There may be no time to learn philosophy, music or poetry for the sake of it, there may be no survival need for it. The knowledgeable human of tomorrow will be exclusively technical. Technology is all he will know and will be enough to earn him a living. The probable creative paralysis of tomorrow will mean that all new knowledge will be purely logical. What the alpharean cannot measure, sense or define will be ignored, permanently deleted and done with somehow. The alpharean's addiction to gadgetry and technology will not help knowledge preservation. Tomorrow, many will trust the cloud with the kind of valuable information and memories that many humans currently keep only in their minds. Many will consult a search engine daily for what the current generation can inherently compute.

The health of the future homo-alpha will not be any better than that of his great predecessors, the current generation. If anything, it may be a little worse. Given the technological sophistication of tomorrow, there will be a drug for anything. A host of ultra-modern medical advances will be available to provide provisional fixes to various ailments and other physical troubles. The circumstance of tomorrow's world will coerce the alpharean into a short term attitude, a myopic mentality. Subsequently, the nature of the alpharean's problem solving methodology will be such that instead of seeking long term ideas, the alpharean will only see benefit in short term workarounds. Instead of endeavouring to permanently heal and eradicate the health problems of the day, the alpharean will rather find temporary remedies to conceal the physical symptoms. These remedies will be convenient to the otherwise ailing and largely unhealthy population.

In other medical matters, Silicon will not just be a boob and bum filler. Botox, face reconstructions and appearance alterations will no longer be a rare luxury exclusive to those with means. Cosmetic wellness will be a thing, balding will be a thing of the past. Alphareans will not count a single baldhead in their midst. Drugs will be redefined and reclassified. There will not be illegal drugs tomorrow. Law enforcement agencies will not have narcotic units and such. The drug of tomorrow will be synthetic and will help with sleep shortening, mood enhancing and fatigue resolution. Organic will be a legacy term as everything else will be *syntho* and lab-made. Despite attempts to control the fat content in his diet, and its effects on body weight; despite other attempts to control the effects of other so-called intoxicants; the Alphareans will still have a good proportion of the unhealthy amongst them. Tomorrow, *foetally invasive* technologies will forecast the future of developing foetuses *inhidvo,* in high definition video. Some brutal governments of tomorrow will determine through some means-testing, who within the national population can be parents and how babies should be made. Numerous children will be products of asexual reproduction; their behaviours and destinies predetermined and pre-programmed before conception. Some children's characters will be manipulated into them before they are babies, *invitro-* in glassy test tubes. Despite the woman of tomorrow's impressive stash of legal dope filling her cabinets, her generation will not be any more inspired than the current sapien woman. The plethora of face realignments, stimulants and sedatives Alphareans will readily have access to will only serve to hide his sad face, mask his daily pain and ready him for another difficult day in the Alpha century.

Of wars and rumours of wars, the super-power of tomorrow will produce and possess weapons of global destruction; weapons whose power of destruction reaches almost everywhere immediately after detonation; self-destructive weapons, weapons of self-destruction. The man of today only wishes that the future generation is sensible enough to avoid war. It will not be an ideal world but it will be advanced. These advances however, do not include ability to pre-empt war and disaster. Unless tomorrow's society attains equality in multiple aspects of everyday living, the threat of war igniting conflict remains realistic. If it happens, the next world war will not be any less significant than the previous world wars. Sick of the previous generation's order, tomorrow's man may revolt into a new world order. The existing order and peace seems a little fragile, but its generation is a little stressed to lead a successful revolution. Luckily, tomorrow's generation will have artificial intelligence. Artificial intelligence will detect the imbalance of power and just might attempt to induce some balance. Tomorrow, it is going to be very hot in some parts of the world. In other parts it will be cold, very cold.

33. Recursion

Recursion was written to mark an individual stubbornness and insistence on the fulfilment of something bigger, better and greater. In a *Recursion*, things get done, redone and redone some more until they are done the way they have to be done. *Recursion* is anytime, anywhere, whether the condition is favourable or not, despite opposing winds, over and over, recursion must persist. *Recursion* is about never stopping until *state zeta* is attained.

Recursion

Recursion is an important element of consistency. Within recursion, exists a form of repeatability. This repeatability helps to exploit convenient coincidences, the kind that most would prefer over the less favourable and loathed inconvenient accidents. In a properly assembled recursion lies a stubborn consistency, a resolute regularity and steady constancy. Recursion is about only fearing fear itself, and letting only the fear of fear be a personal obsession.

Through recursions, the motive for an undertaking evolves. It reappears in different configurations each time. It could be some demonstration of will this time and the motivation to forge on despite situations the next time. Recursion allows for flow of endurance, recursion holds firmly to the *charactery-stick* of consistency. Persistence is another stick recursion sticks to. Reliability is another attribute repeatedly attributed to recursion. Come what may, recursion does it again and again. Whatever condition, recursion ensures that it gets done, whatever needs to be done, however many takes it takes.

Contrary to popular belief, the condition for recursion does not have to be consistent at each epoch. Recursion is not reliant on condition, recursion persists despite condition. In one condition, things may be harder; circumstances may just be a little more difficult than at the time of a previous conquer; darker clouds may have concealed a bright sky; the vibe may be a little uninviting; connectionists may have deliberately disconnected; it may all be unnerving but recursion forges ahead. Recursion warrants that irrespective of condition, and as brief as it avails, opportunity is to be taken advantage of. What the recursion has to continually feed is the fire, the indescribable hunger, the deep belief in the bigger picture, one's pain and one's love. These in-turn, help the cause of recursion.

In one setting, envy stares may be a little more concentrated; acquaintance may have run out of the little patience she pretended to have; but this is alright. In another setting, one may be burdened with depressing events and injustices by seemingly untouchable mortals; this is also alright. Despite the weight and pressures, recursion stands and makes certain that it is so- whatever it is. In a recursion, persistence is self-assured repeatedly. It has to be; it is a matter of life and death. So come what may; situation, struggle, fatigue, pressure, anger, disappointment, name it, whatever it may be. It may be negative, positive, uplifting and depressing; whatever it is, recursion ensures that persistence takes precedence and that a cause is pursued. No matter the favourability or lack, despite opposing winds, over and over, recursion persists.

Be consistent therefore, persist in whatever passions enable you to advance your noble causes, whatever these may be. In persistence be informed also, that it is not always effortless, forces of nature are not ever favourable, conditions are not always conducive. Beware that understanding and tolerance will not always be resident in your neighbour. Understand that your fellowman may not always be cooperative. Your acquaintance's patience is finite and occasionally runs out. But know this also, that opportunity in an unfavourable state must be pursued as purposefully as opportunity in any other setting. To demonstrate the recursive mentality of persistence demands this much. The attitude of recursion demands this much.

Consistently apply the constancy and the confident steadiness of noble ambition to make sure it that your life gets lived your way. But with humility, seek forgiveness from your neighbour. From the same neighbour, I request understanding so that my seemingly arrogant confidence is pardoned. Drunk with illusions of noble causes, my ambition routinely advances its motives above the neighbourhood that acquaints us; me and my neighbour. I know it seems unfair that I find it opportune to undertake an act of recursion when I should be conversing, discussing and interacting with my acquaintance. It is to you acquaintance, that the described forgiveness is sought. Forgive me young friend but understand that recursion never stops.

34. African Scholar

African Scholar is inspired by Ralph Waldo Emerson's American Scholar essay which was reportedly delivered in a speech to the *Phi Beta Kappa* society at Cambridge in 1837. The *African scholar* is about identity and relevance. The piece describes issues of relevance that the scholar is struggling with. Ralph Emerson concluded his *American Scholar* by stating that a nation of men will for the first time exist, because each believes himself inspired by the divine soul. The same could not be any truer for the *African Scholar*. The piece was written to stimulate African men and women who will rise because each believes themselves inspired.

African Scholar

The troubles of the scholar are multiple, among them identity, purpose and relevance. Who and what is relevant to the scholar are some of the smaller issues of the scholar's main problem. The scholar's greater problem is the confusion with whether relevance is of the essence.

The entire value of scholarship is rarely immediately material. It usually takes a while to realise all of it. Although the value of scholarship has never just been commercial, it has afforded certain keen scholars some comfort. The value and relevance of scholarship is ultimately personal; what matters to the scholar decides their perspective on this matter. It is unfortunate that fellow scholars occasionally ridicule one another on the matter of relevance. Each party only knows and argues their perspective, which is usually exclusively supportive to their personal perspective and insensitive to alternative views. In this instance, the arguing parties are seldom relevant to one another unless they are decisively on a similar perspective or choose to be open to another's chosen yet dissimilar view. Just as sanity and insanity need to have a certain compromise to progressively co-exist, the relevance of one's scholarship relative to another hinges primarily on one's acceptance of the other's divergent perspective. But when the scholar is unable to express, embody or live their personal brand in any way, then such is madness.

Usually stereotyped and presumed known before they self-reveal, the African scholar apparently usually has a typical story, rags to middle class, as if it is a unique story. Middle class is better than rags for most, middle class is what is largely acceptable as success to many.

This is not the case for some an African scholar. This African scholar has purpose and constantly strives to align all occupations to this purpose. Purpose, according to the scholar is but a self-generated sense of usefulness to one's people, however many. Informed by young experience and driven by brave ambition, the scholar sets about chasing this purpose. Understanding that not all purposes are conceived equal, the scholar worries not about the size or significance of his purpose. Any purpose is significant enough if it serves value to a neighbour. Most of the time however there appears to be some awareness of this principle by the scholar, and fellow African scholars. Sufficient ambition and insufficient understanding usually requires more effort from the purposeful scholar. In such a circumstance, the purposeful scholar is furnished with little understanding to effectively plan and execute activities demanded by their ambition for the cause of their purpose. And so the massive effort required to pursue the purpose frustrates the scholar. In his frustration, he envies the fellow who lives their brand, the African scholar who invests whatever effort is required to pursue his purpose.

A sense of belonging is essential for the African scholar's confidence, especially when he is in alien territory. The right to mass organise and congregate is one that many times, the African scholar abuses. So when the masses of African scholars gather under some guise and none in the congregation including the convenors identify with the said guise, it is unfortunate. It is not wrong to gather for any reason, but surely many of these an African scholars must have purpose to pursue. Why should the scholar with purpose to pursue decide to kill time? Is it so one can benchmark with fellows and reconfigure if *need* and *will* be? Is it so that the young and aspiring can pay respect to the irrelevant veteran? Considering for a moment that some extraordinary reverence was due to the veteran, what would form the basis of such respect? Is it his subscription to half-baked and conflicting philosophies evidenced by the irrelevance of his conduct? Is it his ill-informed sense of comfort noticeable from his skewed priorities? Or could it just be the veteran's age relative to the young and aspiring? Beyond the usual respect due to all men, no more is due to the veteran. His age comprises memories of missed opportunities and unexplored dreams. He is old but he still wonders the wonder of the young; what it all means. Why then should there be disparity in respect between the irrelevant veteran and the young and aspiring? Age alone cannot be a basis of this extraordinary respect. An old African proverb commands that *susu ilela suswane*; that the old deaf be sensitive to the young deaf; that the old respects the young.

Africa or scholar, which of the two gets precedence in the context of purpose. Is it Africa first then the scholar or the scholar then Africa? Is it both at once? The scholar must decide. But who the scholar is what Africa is to them will help decide the priority and resolve dilemma of Africa and the scholar. The scholar must enquire what this Africa is. Is it the land or the people? Is it both or neither? The African scholar must decide. Whatever the scholar decides determines the way they interact with and realise the idea of African homage, or precisely homage to Africa. Is it impossible that the only right perception of this Africa is strict and narrow? Is it possible that this sole right perception of what it means to be the African scholar is neither inclusive nor accepting of alternative perspectives? What if the acceptance of this single view disables

178

one's objectivity and sensitivity to any other perspective beyond the adopted perception? This is the scholar's confusion. This is why the African scholar constantly conflicts with his fellow. The scholar and fellow conflict frequently because each fails and sometimes refuses to see what his fellow sees. Scholar and fellow regularly conflict because each insists on their view and denies the view of the other. The scholar has learnt that logic does not always host truth and occasionally thinks outside the box. Meanwhile, the fellow is frustrated that the scholar is anything but logical. And this, is usually the origin of the clash of their perspectives, incorrect presumptions. The scholar and fellow do not understand that their paths only cross temporarily and eventually merge into commonality.

The African scholar owes it to Africa. The African scholar is duty bound to give some effort for Africa. This effort, is the effort for African homage. It is not an African way of homage but is a homage for Africa. As wide and varied as Africa is, personal perspective will have to accommodate alternative views. This is the grand principle if any effort to the enrichment of Africa is to be meaningful. Any effort committed to this cause could never be insignificant and this has held, still holds and will hold true for times and ages. It has to start with the mindset, the state of mind has to be set right no matter how beaten, injured and victimised by circumstance the African scholar is. If he perceives it not, how can the African scholar behold and spread hope? If she dreams it not, how can she and others like her live the dream? If a mind is in the right place, it *seeth* not the wrong things; It neither *sayeth* nor *doeth* the wrong thing.

When the trends of the times trouble the African scholar, he must review and affirm the relevance of his scholarship. She must acknowledge the presence of envy the moment the less sophisticated signs of it appear. He must realise counsel and heed to it. She must be humbled by respect and must reciprocate. When game appears, the scholar must recognise a good serve and return without fail. When distraction threatens the African scholar, he must detour not from the cause. It is a noble cause, logic dictates it, circumstance has inspired it, chance has permitted it and time has allowed it. When threatened by strong gale, the African scholar may sway and wave but must not be displaced. When the scholar's purpose is threatened by friend, then friend is foe. The scholar must at all times have the grace to accept the realities and all their kinds. At anytime, the African scholar must be focused enough to withstand the tribulations and must know that fear precedes understanding. As strong as may appear to be, the scholar must remember that fear is not enduring.

The troubles of Africa have been seen and heard far and wide. Far and wide will be the reach of the relevance of the African scholar. His relevance will resonate, her gender will not matter. Who he sleeps with will be unimportant. Her age will be irrelevant, so will be his skin colour and her status. With a perspective that is conscious to alternative thought, the relevance of the African scholar will not be lost. The scholar's relevance will forever remain valid because he is decisively hinged on a perspective that is accommodating to varied views. Her relevance will reach far and wide, not because she does not fear, she accepts fear and transforms it into enduring understanding and courage. Without tiring, the African scholar must constantly battle and constantly defeat the fierce enemy of self and the inconvenience of fear. And when distraction threatens the African scholar, he must detour not from the cause, it is a noble cause.

35. Day of Life

What day is one's best day? Is it the day one conceives of an idea or the day the idea materialises? For some, the best day is the day of the birth of the idea. For some, the best day is the doing day, the day the idea was acted upon. Others would rather their best day be the day they enjoy the rewards of the successful idea. Whatever day it is, the day before it is also a part of the story of the day of one's life. Sometimes the events and circumstances of our daily living condition us to fixate on the destination and short term outcome. Occasionally we get accustomed to paying little regard to the significance of the journey and the process. The process counts, the process is how an idea gets clearer with each day and also how an idea becomes more convoluted as the days pass.

Day of Life

Beautiful moment is what a particular moment exactly was that Sunday. It was a Sunday one will probably never forget. Blessed Sunday, it surely was too. A little delay and sufficient digress has to be paid in respect to that moment that Sunday. It was a good Sunday, weather must have been good, one recalls it being a pleasant weather. But one knows for sure that it was a day to remember. It was on that Sunday that one rested; and it was while resting that one paused for a moment. And there in the midst of the pause, one disentangled it. There it was, real but abstract yet illusory and mental. Finally, one had figured it out, one had *overstood* it. In that pause when one unravelled it, it was a beautiful moment. One recalls that one smiled to oneself in that moment. One realised that had one not rested and paused, had one just kept at it, whatever it was; one would not have been refreshed. That Sunday was the day after a hectic Saturday. Had one been unrefreshed and laden in tiredness, one would not have woken to such inspired imagination. One needed to rest that Sunday thanks to the previous Saturday night.

The Saturday before that Sunday was by far one of the best of one's best days. Not a typical Saturday by any standards, it was super; one decided it was so when one got up. Despite the hangover from the previous Friday night's romp, it was a memorable Saturday. It was the Saturday that one had seriously thought about it. For the entire day, as one went about his Saturday chores, one repeatedly spared a moment or two to the thought. At each moment, the thinking became more focussed than before. Occasionally in these moments, brief trances of deep involuntary mental brainstorming would transform one to a different state of mind. One did not mind this state of mind. One knew that it could not get any better than the occasional mental transformations on a splendid Saturday. So one appreciated that the Saturday's mental transformations were a rare treat; the thinking was inspired by the previous Friday's perception. The splendid-ness of Saturday had continued from the previous Friday. Had one not perceived it that Friday, one would not have thought so deep and so repeatedly about it on that Saturday. It was a great day that Saturday but the Friday before it had not been uneventful. It had been an *all right-all day-all night* kind of Friday.

How could one forget Friday? Freaks' Friday, funky-feisty Friday, it was the day of the night of lights. The lights of acumen were on that Friday night; it was unlike any other. It was a night of the gods, a night of temptation; that Friday night was a night of a little indulgence. It was in one such brief indulgence that one perceived it. One could almost visualize it. It was gradually coming together. It was not quite clear but in a perceivable state. One remembered a saying about perception preceding appreciation and that visualization *precurses* actualisation. So one figured that the Friday perception must have been headed somewhere. To one, the perception in that momentary indulgence must have had some importance. Combined with the events of Thursday, the meaning of the perception on Friday became a little clearer. The events of Thursday had been catalyst to the great perception on Friday. Had one not had them imaginings on Thursday, the Friday perception might not have been. The events of Friday were starting to make sense but it had all started the day before on Thursday.

The Thursday had come and gone fast. It must have
been due to the day's hectic proceedings. It was a
touch and go day, a *bee-busy-ness* kind of day. One
never forgot that Thursday; it had a buzz about it. It
was an inspired Thursday, the air was pregnant with
mystique, anything could happen, and on that day,
that Thursday, that day of *Thor* and *Thoth*, something
did happen.   That day, a thunderous thought kept
bugging one, one kept being interrupted by this
recurring   imaginations.   There   was   this   one
particularly persistent imagination; it took one on a
wondrous wander. It had gone on for two days and
had started the day before, on the Wednesday. It may
not have continued on Thursday had one stopped it on
Wednesday. One vividly remembers how it started the
day before that Thursday on Wednesday.

Wednesday started fine. One has good memories of
that sweet Wednesday; off the bed just after six,
quickie, young morning stretch, short run to and from,
a candid reflection while at it, catch the sun rising,
hasty shower and an apple to break the fast. It did not
feel like a Wednesday, one had the energy of a Monday
and the *restedness* of a Sunday. The day had gone
unsurprisingly well. The Monday-like energy sustained
through the day and the faux Sunday restedness
endured for most of the day. Despite the liveliness and
all the freshness, a strange imagination formed and
stayed on one's mind. What was this thing one was
imagining? Was it a future event, an idea? One could
not quite figure it out but it was there and would not
go away, one kept imagining it. Why couldn't it just be
clear? One decided to not worry about it further that
Wednesday. Strangely, it had some similarities to the
previous night's dream. Tuesday night's dream had
disturbed one throughout the night. It had not been a
sleepy night but it helped one to get up early and sieze

the Wednesday. It turned out to be a sweet Wednesday but what a Tuesday it had been.

Tuesday was quiet and typical of one's Tuesdays. One recalls the general calm of that particular Tuesday. Eerily quiet Tuesday it was too. Still winds, cool, overcast day. It was no day of inspiration, not that Tuesday. It was a day to live all the same. It was a day to just do it, and do it one attempted. By evening, it turned out to have been a productive Tuesday. The just do it attitude had been useful once more. And the night, it was a nice Tuesday night, one hit the sheets at the usual time, just after a cuppa, just before midnight. In his sleep one had a dream; except that dream was no typical dream. Tuesday's dream was different. One had been wallowing in confusion all night, wondering what the dream meant. Could it be something to do with the overcast and eeriness of that Tuesday? - one wondered. Not all Tuesdays could be like that Tuesday. Certainly no other dream was like the Tuesday dream. But what it meant and where it had come from was a mystery. Could it be some indirect reflection from the previous Monday's events? Had one's Monday's blues spilled into the usually peaceful Tuesday night's sleep? Damn the Monday blues. They were probably a cause for Tuesday's baffling dream.

Damned Monday, the day before it started. Actually the Monday is the day it all started. Damned Monday, the dreaded day, the most remembered Monday, one's greatest Monday. One hates it; one hates to repeat that it was a *damned good* Monday but it was a damned good Monday. Nobody could hate that Monday. Nobody could hate a day like that Monday, not when the day is as memorable as that Monday. That Monday is the best Monday one has ever lived through. Although it created its own blues, it was the

Monday that one decided would not be blue. Either by hook or crook, it had to be a proper productive Monday. That Monday, one had things to do. Towards the end of that busy Monday, one stopped work for the day. After a meal, a drink and some *do-be*, one set-back, lounged and appreciated the toil of the day, recalled the efforts, heroics, luck and magic of the previous Sunday. Sunday had been the day to get it. Sunday was the day it had unravelled. The Monday had certainly felt different, unlike the usual blue Mondays. However, had one not figured it out that previous Sunday, the Monday would surely have been blue. Beautiful day was what it was that Sunday. It certainly was a Sunday one will probably never forget. Blessed Sunday, it was too.

36. Bye World

Bye World is a note of exit. The narrative recalls the awesome and awful events and experiences of the world; how some of them will be missed and how some will never be experienced anymore. The note is supposedly written from beyond the physical life, the writer declares being past the physical world. In one part the writer describes themselves as gone and beyond the worldly troubles and hardship. The uncertainty of the writer's new found relief beyond the physical world is also apparent, although more than once, the piece questions the permanence of the realm beyond the known world.

Bye World

World, fare thee well. Gone is this self. I am gone, never to return. Farewell world; I am out, out of this world. This is it, my exit. Stay well world. Your welcome to celebrate me but don't mourn me. This much I know I have earned. Don't you mourn me.

Bye world, I am gone. I have escaped your troubles. I have sought and found relief to your pressures. I am beyond the hardship I endured under your conditions. I am over the bitterness and above the unpleasant. My newly found let-live attitude may be brief but the killer attitude is a mentality I need no more. For now, I am over the struggles; I am done with the hustling, the striving, blood and sweat shed in the toil. This is it world. I have transcended; having come from nothing, back to nothingness I have returned. I am not of this world anymore. I am gone.

Goodbye world, I will miss you. I will miss your simple pleasures, your passions, the twisted, innocent and deep passions. These, I will probably miss the most. The few I was privileged to experience, the sadder it has been to let go of their savour. I will miss your worldly experiences. These were amazing at their best and inspiring at their worst. I now certainly know that all were worth it, every one of them. I remember each of these experiences fondly, the ones that made me sick in the gut included. I will miss your times world, mornings the most. My mornings were the best times. A fair few of my best moments occurred in the mornings. As for the afternoons, they were magnificent. Afternoons were my normal times. They were my up an about times. These were my times to interact with the world and whenever I could, wander briefly into the wondrous. And the nights, the nights were romantic and sobering, dreamy and nightmarish. Most of my nights were optimistic, spent mostly in positivity, pondering at the half-fullness of my life glass. Every several nights, a couple of pessimistic thoughts would gather into a nightmare while I slept. It was usually either just random thoughts or consequent to an earlier experience. Sometimes, the negative thought would eventually unravel into an opportunity for courage and self-assurance. Sometimes, the scary thought would provide a stimulus to scream to the gods. Despite the nightmares, I will miss my nights still. My nights were not just my times for reminiscing, I had my own *Ella* to kiss too. But now I am gone. No longer will there be time, existence seems infinite and formless in my new realm. I will miss your summers, my *out in the sun* days, my times of fun. The memories of your winters will stay with me; cold but not freezing; shivering but not still. I am stronger for them.

Farewell world, I have left. I hopefully I have left you in peace. Hopefully I stole none of your peace, however little of it was left. I hope my brief existence did not drain any of your little, diminishing love. I hope you hold on to it, nurture it too. I hope you use it for noble purposes and are generous with it. I hope you see a neighbour's good through it. I found some love in you world. I gave some and got some back. I have also hated and have wished ill on others. Hell, I even entertained some schadenfreude at some of their troubles. Eventually, I forgave and wished ill no more. I have wished some dead and done with. I thought the irritation they represented and caused demanded it. For these too, I would ultimately embrace good and forgiveness. Some re-offended and were re-forgiven, some were dealt with in a compensatory manner, and then they too were forgiven. I know I have been wished ill too and I hope I too have been forgiven. If I irritated you world, I apologise. If I caused you to wish me dead, then *mea culpa mundo*. I am gone but I am not dead yet; lest you drown in guilt for thinking your evil thought caused my seeming death. Worry not, you could never hurt me. I know you can't help it, you can't help not worrying. But if it helps, just know that it's not your fault that I am not dead, I am just gone.

Bye world! You may forget me but you probably won't forget about me. You will forget not what I stood for. Remember always what I chose to represent, what I identified with, what I lived for, what I was prepared to die for and what I died for. Asking you to remember me may be selfish, but pleading that you forget not the cause, our cause, is not far from selfless. I am gone now; never will I be seen and touched. The physical cannot perceive me anymore, the conventional can't make sense of me. I am now physically unreal, I am not actual to the superficial. But I know you still hear my word. I know that though I am gone you still get my concept. Goodbye world. Stay well. I hope you remember our fine interactions, I trust you cherish our conflicts, no matter how mutually inconvenient they were at times. I know you know that I tried. I tried to be me- tried to do what I wanted to, tried to say what I felt. I know you know full well that I tried to be what I said I was about. For that I know that though you may forget me, you will not forget about me. About me, you will remember that my cause was my cross, that my meditations only sought peace and that my words, although illogical sometimes, attempted to decipher the truth of all-time. Bye world, I know you know that though I be gone, I still be here.

So long world; I hope to see you again. I hope we meet again. I hope also that the next time is as engaging as the previous time, our first time. Hopefully the next time we meet is as inspiring and as trying as the previous. From where I am now, I mostly miss you but sometimes I wish we never met. At times, I think about how I have had enough of you, enough of your pressures and problems. Your hardships and sufferings, I don't want to have to endure them anymore. Who would? Maybe one who has strived and thrived on struggle, a mortal who came, saw and conquered. Or maybe a mere man who tried, tried again, kept trying and died trying still. Such is the capacity of one who would be gone from you and still miss you world. One who appreciates that though you may be full of trouble, accident, vulnerability and disaster; you are also hopeful, inspiring and worth living for, worth living in. Goodbye world, I will miss you. Or maybe not.

37. Cause of Effect

Cause of Effect is a way of thinking that proposes that any two items are not an effect of, but only a result of summing the individual items. The same thinking proposes that although one's destiny can be defined by their circumstance, the circumstance is not all that determines one's destiny. The piece is deep, good food for thought. In another analogy, the *Cause of Effect* proposes that happiness is not the effect of giving but it can result from an act of giving. The idea of the *Cause of Effect* is that there is hardly a single cause to an effect, the individual determines the other cause. Shape your causes to your effects.

Cause of Effect

Two items summed together are not the effect of summing the two individual units but are a possible result of the summation. In a similar manner, an individual can be the way they are because of their situational conditions, but their conditions are not all that influence who the individual becomes. There can never be one cause of effect. Numerous other causes with the power of effect exist around any situation.

In search of accomplishment, a writer writes a book, if it is easily understood and resonates with the masses, it will sell. As long as it is popular, it is enough for the writer. In search of impact, a thinker shares insight. It has to affect whomever it reaches. As long as it is relevant, this is enough for the thinker. The writer knows that words are thoughts, no matter how randomly scrambled. They may communicate an alternate thought, but thought still. The thinker knows that a chaser of great ambition is only happy while they chase. The feeling of closing in on the fleeting goal, this is what makes the chaser happy. It may not matter if the writer's book does not sell but it matters if the thinker's insight is irrelevant. The accomplishment badly sought may never be found, the vanity thirst may never be completely quenched, but the impact has to be effected. The writer has to keep writing, the thinker has to stay on the train of thought. This may not be the only cause but will prompt the desired effect.

Happiness is not the effect of giving but can result from it, for both the giver and the given. A heartfelt gift always touches. It may not impress with its not so bright coloured wrapping. It may not have the top scent and may not be marketed under some grand brand. The gift of passion is guaranteed to affect, one way or the other. The ultimate gift, is rarely further than the giving of self. The selfless gift is usually borne of one's labours, the professional, mental, physiological, mystical and alternate labours. But if the gift does not fascinate and has no dazzle, what guarantees it to touch and move the given? It will be felt, this is from where it acquires the touch effect. It will be deeply understood and badly mistaken. It will be imagined, pictured even. It will be figured out, misconstrued at times. It will be a long ramble, a short fact sometimes. It will be beautifully ambiguous to some, scaringly precise to others. It will be written on paper, sung in music and taught to knowledge seekers. This is how it touches. This is how it causes its effect.

For survival, to get by, to thrive, for other different causes, the populace is busy. The poor search for the illusive comfort. Some give up and accept their pauper status. Some get fed up with the system and mass revolt. Some push themselves and excel. Whereas some watch others and wish they too would get rich as fast. Some just don't bother. Meanwhile some write it down, hoping it all comes together some day. Sowing a seed at a time, counting on the mathematics of multiplication; expressing a thought at a time, relying on the philosophy of small beginnings; giving it their all, hoping for the magic of luck. For dominance, for greatness, for ruthlessness and for *farksake*, the world engages and commits, the world marks, divides, owns and excludes. For whatever reason, the world hurts; domination of nations, companies, ethnicities, cultures and ideas over fellows is commonplace. To thrive, some try and strive; for riches, others hoard and accumulate. For joy, some give it all away, conscripted into simple living. In pursuit of a cause and some accomplishment, one expresses insight. This *ex-*

pression is exigent since insight is *ex-sential* to the effect of mass enlightenment. It may not be the only cause but insight is a possible cause of the effect of enlightenment.

This is the effect, our world is diverse, our varieties and diversities are overwhelming our similarities. The effect is, we have become competitors and life is a great contest for survival. To the effect of survival, collaborations are forged, contracts are agreed and signed; for some aspect of survival, plans and budgets are put in place; defences are tested and attacks are launched. The effect is, some are hurt, some are happy, some win, some lose, some prosper, some languish, some are ignorant, some claim to be informed but still don't know. The effect is, none is certain what they really are, who they really are. Some do not care, some do, some live it up and some live from day to day. Yet some try and figure it out, the way out, some try and fail and try again. This is the effect and state of our diverse world. The population is consistently engaged in the struggle for self-preservation. In this quest some take more and give less. To give it a less morally deficient effect, they call this act efficiency. Its other effect is the effect of selfishness, the effect of miserliness. Stinginess cannot be a viable cause to happiness, even in a desperate and competitive world. For the effect of happiness, there are other several inclusive causes. To any effect, there can never be just one cause.

38. Khun Anup

The legend of *Khun Anup* is about eloquence, about diamonds in rubbles, it is about beauty in unusual places. The piece is based on the story of Khun Anup, a peasant in ancient Egypt. The piece retells the story of Khun Anup with a theme that even among peasants can be found the extraordinary. In the piece, peasants are urged to be confident in the knowledge that history is never complete without them. The story of Khun Anup is the story of and for eloquent peasants, the ones that great stories depend on to be told in truthful flair. Meanwhile, a story told to its completion leaves the audience little room for imagination.

Khun Anup

For all in peasantry, for a special time when flair stands out in simple truth.

The legend of Khun Anup is popular for the supposed eloquence of Khun Anup the peasant. His eloquence was apparently discovered at a time when he was probably at his lowest point emotionally. When his eloquence unravelled, Khun must have been afraid, worried and miserable. The man, according to some version of this legend, was appearing for trial and was in trouble with the pharaohs, the authorities of the time. The man's immediate interest at the time was to get out of the trouble into which he found himself immersed, the story suggests such. According to the legend, Khun Anup was under immense pressure; given the circumstances, the stress he must have been under is not difficult to imagine. An alternative analogy summarises what may have been Khun Anup's slimmest chance out of the ancient Egyptian capital punishment; that just as guts are revealed when any being is pressed; truth comes out when sufficiently pressed out of an individual. This analogy implies that internal pressure and calamity should not always be frowned upon, especially when unprovoked. Such a period indicate the climax of an incubation of one's brilliance. Thus the brilliance of Khun Anup became apparent at a time of immense pressure.

The few who identify with the legend of Khun Anup are best suited to advise on whether it is wise to reveal one's brilliance when one is at their lowest. It does not seem unwise to involuntarily use one's difficult moment to show one's true grit. One can relate to how the easiest time to be one's true self is the moment when one is most desperate. There cannot be many other better situations to be legendary. Unless one is a perfect faker, there can't be that many people with the skill and neck to fake who they are not in a desperate moment. Being one's true self is sustainable and for most, the default position in times of need. Being one's self may well be the easiest state to be in at the hardest of times. It may be regrettable and embarrassing is some situations but it is essential in all circumstances. The brilliance of Khun Anup in a difficult situation may have had something to do with the type and kind of peasant he was. If the brilliance he displayed at his trial was not who he was then he must have summoned all faking energies he could afford and it still could have backfired. Given the context of the legend, Khun Anup was no fake, he stayed true to his self and turned out to be a symbol of eloquence.

Decades later, Khun Anup has been numerously referred to as the eloquent peasant. The existence of eloquence in peasantry in the legend of Khun Anup was shocking and uncommon at the time in ancient Egypt. According to common knowledge of the time, eloquence and peasantry were logically distant and socially unrelated. Any relation of the two in any way was bound to raise eyebrows and attract scorn from the elite. Despite social norms, relating eloquence and peasantry was the soreness that the legend of Khun Anup aggravated on the rulers of ancient Egypt. The story of Khun Anup defied the conventional stereotype and challenged established convention. The faint distinction between good and bad, ugly and pretty, the thin line between strong and weak, rich and poor and the relativity of brilliance and dullness were exposed by the legend of Khun Anup. In conflating eloquence and peasantry, the eloquence of Khun *murkied* the establishment's sensitivity to the fragile differences and overlaps of two supposed extremes. Ultimately, the story of Khun made acceptable the interactivity and parallel existence of opposites in a single realm. According to the story, many who thought they knew realised they knew nothing. Many who thought that they *were* realised that they *weren't*. Those whom the story socially inconvenienced came to the realisation that power and wealth is not entirely in material possessions. Finally, they began to accept that the eloquence of Khun Anup was innately his. They accepted that he just had it in him.

Peasants of Egypt at the time of Khun Anup and elsewhere where the legend penetrated must have celebrated the glory of a fellow peasant. Being peasant, they would have probably related and felt ownership to the story, they must have felt some temporary relief, some glimpse of hope must have flashed before them. They must have felt good for Khun Anup and with themselves. As for the man, he must have lived happily ever after. The system would have probably absorbed him into its structures. Availed at his disposal would have been a couple or several peasants to attend to his needs and wants. He, a former peasant would have then had some of his own peasants. Probably born of good and being good inherently, Khun would have remained true to his self and maintained relevance to the good people, the peasants. He would have refused all that made him different to those he identified with.

Peasants who heard of Khun Anup's fortunes must have felt some pride for one of theirs. The revolution represented by Khun Anup was probably spread by word of mouth in hushed tones. Broadcasting a peasant's eloquence may have been a violation of some code set by the ruling powers at the time. The fact that the legend survived for so long is uncharacteristic of the response by the ruling system to any personification of heroism by peasants. Heroism under the regime would have been exclusively synonymous with the ruling elite. Despite the difficult conditions of the early retellers, the story was retold repeatedly and the legend of Khun Anup lives centuries later. Peasants one and all must have felt inspired, they must have felt the significance of such rarity. None of them would have felt any shame in identifying and relating to the nobility of a fellow peasant. Very well represented is how they must have felt. The peasants' common thought that the brilliance of one peasant is the brilliance of all would have been sufficient to sustain the peasants' empathy with the heroics of Khun.

It would have been unimaginable to the elite that eloquent peasants were in existence during the time of Khun Anup. Khun may have been one of a kind, a rare find, one in a million even but one of the millions still. There would have been many who identified with Khun Anup prior to the discovery of his eloquence at his trial. There would have been many others whom Khun regarded as being in the same chain as himself. It would have been a rare probability that his eloquence would be eventually discovered, let alone the way his path to heroism unravelled. The peasants must have taken a bow in their numbers then, they probably did, comfortable in the good old peasant confidence that their story will find resonance, achieve relevance and remain legendary.

At a time when it was most unsupportive to do so, Khun never stopped wishing and working for better. In his only known writing, Khun Anup writes that it is not a shame to wish for better. He advises that it is a shame however, if one wishes for better but the wish is not accompanied by a readiness, a *can-do* and *will-do* attitude. Khun asserts that this is what is almost always necessary to actualise desires.

On simplicity, Khun comments that simpleness is subjective, that each understands in their own way if they are simple and how simple they are. Khun also proposes that when a recurring urge to do better and be better troubles and bothers one; and provided one is a can do, will do and does do kind of peasant; then even if one finds themselves in uncomfortable positions, it must not trouble one since this is one's opportunity to demonstrate eloquence, to just be. At this time of supposed need, Khun suggests one can only be their true self. This, according to Khun is all one can be and actually be. In concluding Khun writes that when the peasant is suddenly called eloquent following a display of eloquence, it is not who they have suddenly become but all they have ever been.

39. Heat of the Moment

If Abstraxion was a book of songs, *Heat of the Moment* would be the first song. The heat of the moment is the precise condition in which each piece of Abstraxion was written. This heat of the moment is the moment to do it, whatever it is. Some call it impulse, others know it as spontaneity, Latins named it *promptu*, old Greek gods refer to it as *naturel*. To many, it is the heat of the moment. There is no better time than now. Think now of the inequality of everything, the unfairness of anything; think now of any other troubles around you. Think about what you can do about it. Remember and be grateful now also, for the good things in your perfect life. And so do whatever you can now. Act now, live now because your life is spent in multiples of momentary *nows*, ever fleeting. In the *Heat of the moment* put your now to good use, now.

Heat of the Moment

In the end every man is for himself. One man fights, one man flees. What one does is up to one, voluntary or not, some decision must be made. So when *push meets shove*, one needs not forget one's friendships, partnerships, faculties and capabilities. When the moment calls it and one has to deploy; confidently knowing that one can, one goes ahead, wrestles it and conquers it, one is all over it. The victory is overwhelming. Asked to describe the feeling, one is out of words, blames it on the heat of the moment.

Conventional beauty is usually not hard to miss and easily *spotable*. Inner beauty is the exact opposite, harder to recognise and even harder to tame. But some odd day for some inspired duration, the relevant variables accidentally converge and inner beauty is responsive. This is not a moment to be wasted so hurry ye-self. Hopefully ye been preparing for times such as this; so that when the right conditions are momentarily in place, then ye shall tarry not. Appreciating the rarity of the opportunity, rush not ye-self but be ye urgent. This is the time to tame inspired beauty, albeit momentarily. It is finally here, the time to act. Some call it impulse, spontaneity, ancient Latins called it promptu, Zeus and Tyche referred to it as *naturel*, to many, it is only the heat of the moment.

The average man works hard; the average woman also so. Usually a victim of circumstance, he has lost all hope. Traditionally a troubled soul, she is inconsolable. Conditioned by situation, he is unforgiving. Scared by history, she is untrusting. Lost his focus, he has become foul. Blinded by sadness, she has grown cold. Hear ye average man, hearken thou average woman; troubled, stressed, depressed, tired, delicate and exhausted is who we all are. Living is why we are here. So when circumstance, condition and history are against, unsupportive and opposite; when all else pulls against; find a time, find time to stand, time to try, time to do, make time to act. Add purpose to existence, define and live your meaning of life, do something. If it fails this time, find another time, try another time, do something, create your heat of the moment.

We are the modern species. Our technology is superior to those of old. We are the modern man; our backs are more upright than those of old. We are the sophisticated beings; we prevail over all others, living and dead. We are the greatest generation; we have been to the moon and space. We are the *neosapien,* most mentally elaborate of all. Our ability to self-organize and self-preserve determines and dictates it; that we are better than all. But are we really? If so how come we cause so much trouble? How come some want more than others? How come others have much more than others? Is this the balance our long term survival needs? What then of the large scale spite and greed? And the wars and rumours of them? And what of this climate change, is it fact of fiction? Apparently our globe is warming. Apparently we will soon be living in perpetual and unrelenting heat. Apparently it will be like nothing we have experienced before, nothing like the heat of the moment.

Romanticists and eroticists allege that the greatest human power is harnessed with the most efficiency when love meets passion. Apparently this power is short-lived, according to this *theorium passos,* the theory of passion. This power, according to the *theorium* overcomes anti progress influences and prevails over the body, mind and soul. It is a powerful power, persisting and prevailing only momentarily. With the powerful power, one can do anything, as long as the powerful power sustains. This power permeates persistently even the hardest of compounds. So anyone under any circumstance best be alert to the supremacy of the impromptu power. Apparently it strikes only in the heat of the moment.

To all speakers, spread the truth, you owe it to the masses. Merchants, find true value, the world will be better for it. Soldiers, fight for justice, lest ye be judged and haunted by bad. Meditators, focus your thoughts, understand the spectrum of perspective. Rebels, find a cause, a selfless cause. *Penners*, pen up, the revolution must be recorded. Twitters and Followers wake up, let your tweet define the better you. Observers, be accurate, history rides on it. Activists be convicted, it may sell better than the falsehood you are representing. Authors, be creative, it is only fair to the average consumer. Writers and thinkers, be relevant, the readership deserves it. Artists, be inspired, a work of passion lives longer. Social medians, quit status posting, live the moment. Learners and scholars, find impact, our world yearns for it. Whoever ye be, *carpe momentum*, realise the power of now, the power of the heat, the heat of the moment.

Life, according to some is a collation of memories, a compilation of *everydays*, a summation of existence, a sum of the moments, each happening at a special time, now. Those who understand this principle understand that in order to have lived, one must dare, one must attempt, one must rather fail than not try. Those who consciously choose to live a life of impact do so with full awareness and little fear for the substantial circumstance obstructing them, they count on the powerful power to permeate, they count on never giving up. It is these who ultimately get it done. They silently hold dear the idea that when one can, one must. For these it has been said many times that they get it, whatever they define it to be. At any moment it may burn them but constantly they endure it. However extreme it may be, it is only a matter of time before it finally gets done. Meanwhile, in between times, before the moment of conquer, it is time to work, time to move it, it is the heat of the moment.

40.Con of Man

The con is alive, the con is illusive, the con is strong. The con is fair, selfish and conscious. The con cares, the con is commercial, the con is uncommon. These are a few of the *con-victions* of the con, the common man. The con is the mystical spirit of Umaru, the philosophical thought of Con Fuseus. Elaborate in abstract, the con is the eloquence of Khun Anup. The con is Khukhi and Nkazi. The con is you, me too. *Con of Man* is a tribute to the con in each of us. Each must know and understand their con. If you have no con, you are not looking hard enough.

.

Con of Man

The con is the common man. The con survives, sells his toil and earns his wage. The con is realist, hopes for the best and prepares for the worst. The con is rugged but rare; not precious but priceless.

Common con.

The con lives ordinarily. He is simple, she is plain. The con goes through the days like the *day-to-day* people. He eats, prays and lives with the common men. She smiles, laughs and cries with the average women. Breathes, hurts and exclaims as they do. Like them, the con tires, rests and recovers.

Con is illusive.

The con is hard to figure out. Has never been obvious, especially to the naked eye. Immeasurable, undetectable, the con is stealthy; neither metric nor technology can quantify con. Focused and meticulous, sloppy and slippery, the con is unpredictable. Here today, there tomorrow, the con is progressive. Appearing momentarily, disappearing instantly, the con is magical, has always been wondrous. Supernatural and unreal, the con cannot be substantiated.

Strong con.

The con is sturdy, industrious in endeavour. The con possesses some power, a *powerful power*. The con persists in this power, stands by this power. Not much is known of the power, except that it is the power of the con. Without it the con would not be a con; and without the con there would not be such power. The power defines the con, such that the con is strong. At the peak of this strength, the con is powerful.

Con is *fellow*.

Generally good and in good standing with his fellow, the con is fair. Fights the good fight, lives and lets fellow live; forgives and tries to forget. The con is sympathetic, celebrates the neighbour's good tidings and weeps at a friend's loss. The con is spiritual, pays tribute to the higher powers, prays several times a day, quotes the bible, swears by the quran and believes in livity. The con is positive, chardi karla is his mantra. The con is obedient, does not get royalty but tolerates royals, acknowledges authority and demands accountability. With his fellow the con cooperates. With her fellow the con shares; the con consults, the con concurs.

The con is selfish.

It is about what's in it for the con. This is the thought of the con once in a while. Looking out for con is another of the con's thoughts. Many have labelled him *con-niving*, but con believes that con serves best when con is selfish. The con is informed; informed that the enemies are those closest. The con understands that every man be for *hisself;* from alternative philosophies, the con has learnt that selfless is overrated, that selfish is inherent, and so the con is selfish.

Con-scious.

The con keeps an open eye. Never lost in spectacular-dazzle, con is always attentive to the reflection of the light. The con is sensitive, aware that to every action is a reaction. That what goes around comes around. The con survives, sells his toil and earns his wage. The con is read, perused the texts of old thinkers. The con is realist, hopes for the best and prepares for the worst. The con is grateful, to those we know nothing of, but swear by, fight for, wrongly hate and kill for, wherever they may be.

The con cares.

The con empathises. If one is sad then con is sad. When one wins, the con wins. The con feels for, the con yearns for. When a friend is in debt, con wishes they could pay it back. The con understands, the con can relate. The longing of ambition, con feels it too. The power of fear, it scares con too. Tired, uninspired, con's been there too. Doing it for the sake of it? done that too. Temptation, con has succumbed to it. When it counts, most times, the con gives; when it matters, all the time, the con cares.

The commercial con.

Con is a brand; trademarked, copyrighted and targeting a particular market. The con is an enterprise, built on passion and ambition. The con sells, worth its value in legal tender. The con is competitive, outsells and outwits competition. The con has market appeal, attracts the masses. The con is profitable, affords the man some value. The con is lucrative, allows the woman some profit. The con is viable, a product for the long term. The con is bankable, quality stock, feasible investment. The con is economic, effective with resources.

Uncommon as the con.

The con is unheard of, neither here nor there. The con is unpopular, both home and away. The con is rugged but rare; not precious but priceless. The con is the uncommon phenomenon, stuff of legends. Life's battles, fought all, won some, lost some, still standing and ready to go. Extraordinary, the con succeeds at all endeavour. Successful with each attempt, this is no general occurrence. Ever inspired, always connected and focused, this cannot be an everyday thing. Strong willed and instinctive, the con is no regular fellow. Dedicated and in it for the long run, the con is not the usual average. Awesome and brilliant at best, exploitative and selfish at worst, this is no standard trend. The con is no common character.

The con is prepared.

The con is ever-ready, alert. The con is ever alert, steady. The con is ever-steady, ready to go. The con is go, the con is green. The con is ever-green, motivated. The con is ever-motivated, persistent. The con is ever-persistent, endures. The con is ever-enduring, purposeful. Endurance is element to purpose sayeth the gods. The con is ever-purposeful, prepared. Prepared for chance, prepared for luck, if ever she shows. Prepared for fate, prepared for prospect; whenever he suffices.

Mystic and con.

Old century, the con is historic. Such and such great deed has been said of con and about con. Visionary, the con is the future. From *nano* to *femto* technology, the con has seen tomorrow. Mystical, the con is the spirit of Umaru. Forever and ever; there is, there was, the con is the continuum. Unknown, the con is a conspiracy. The con is not actually a con; only a con in certain light. This is what makes con *non-con*. Undercover, the con is clandestine; concealed from view and encrypted to the uninformed. An old book, the con is a myth. Modern editions can only translate and extrapolate. None can ever precisely re-tell the tale of con.

41. Teachings of Con Fuseus

Philosopher Con Fuseus is one of the less known but one of the most provocative of old *philosophisers*. Not much is written about the philosopher. His works were a series of brief abstracts challenging the establishment and mocking conventional thinking. Today, books by and about Con Fuseus can hardly be found because most were rounded up and burnt after a group of philosophers plotted to have him silenced. A couple of surviving copies are rumoured to be secretly held by private collectors in known but undisclosed locations. For the same reasons, Con Fuseus has been dismissed by some philosophers as a non-philosopher because his works are not philosophies. Con Fuseus has always maintained that not all philosophers practice philosophy and that not all who practice philosophy are philosophers. This is a claim rebutted as *Con-Fuseunist* by the detractors of Con Fuseus. This piece samples some of the teachings of the philosopher.

Teachings of Con Fuseus

Perfection is vanity but be ye perfectionists.

Kindness is virtuous, most people do not get it; the fool exploits it even when it is meant to benefit them. On the outside, it appears that giving is biased, one sided and done by one person, the giver. However, this giver is not the only giver; they are just the outside giver. There is another giver, the inside giver. The inside giver resides within the outside taker. Each time the outsider gives, their insider receives. Similarly, every time one accepts a physical item, their inside gives something. Every time without fail, this transactional, two sided giving occurs when some gifting takes place. Takers must know that taking is never one sided. For each physical take, the inside gives. It is a personal choice who one chooses to be. Although the superior alternative in this context seems obvious, it is neither position is disadvantageous. Everyone gets something.

Living for the moment is pleasurable. Immediate gains are happy gains. Indulgence for the sake of it may be just what the body and soul need sometimes, the mind may benefit from this too. Times of measured indulgence allow for the stillness to hatch yet another grand plan. In this moment of seeming *zeroness*, the mind may put together a thought or two for one's next great leap; a leap beneficial to the man and his kind. As always, the motive has to be right and the undertaking for noble reasons. Despite the need for occasional pause, *neglect laziness* every so often hides in the hammock of indulgence. For some, this makes it harder to tell measured indulgence and neglect laziness apart. Consequently laziness if kept neglect, intertwines into indulgence and the result is repercussion. This is why it is better to rest tired. Resting while one is refreshed and energetic is unwise and unbeneficial. Resting must follow a good dose of focused work. This way rest and indulgence only serve to provide the required measured respite. And the good dose of work one must complete before rest, it contributes to the toil of the long term. It is important to work and live for now, to be in moment. It is also beneficial to habitually look further than the current, to look into the time to come. Life is not a one thing, it is many things and also naturally sophisticated. Life is also largely interactive, one's interaction with it determines what one gets out of it and also what life gets out of one. Planning is essential, it may be estimated and imprecise but also useful. Living for now is pleasurable but investment in the long term is important, definitely so too.

Life is not a one thing, it is many things. Life is also naturally simple, the living being complicates it. The simplicity of it is that life is for living. As long as each plays their position, teaches and encourages their offspring to follow the mould, then life goes on. As long as each accepts what they are and lives with it, then life is good. Apparently not, long have a people accepted what they are, was life good then? Apparently not. People ultimately get sick of accepting what they are, especially if what they are is not much. Many more have died from accepting what they are. So apparently there is more to life than just getting by. One has to discover who they are. This is all there is to it, this is the simplicity of life. If one attempted to discover who they are or died trying, then life has meaning. If one knows who they and pursues their cause, then life has purpose. The reality is hardly this simple. Life refuses to be abstracted into a simple concept. Life remains stubbornly wondrous, hard, mysterious, fun, cruel, evil, beautiful, inspiring, unforgiving, all at once. The simplicity of life is its sophistication. In the same context, life's simplicity complicates it. Ultimately, only the life context one assumes and pursues must matter.

What then of ambition? It is a prerequisite to personal achievement. All personal achievement is driven by ambition. Ambition is what the travelling evangelist packs first in their baggage. It is what extreme explorers put on before any garment. Ambition is what the writer counts on when penning a provocative line. If anyone lacks ambition, they may also not have purpose. Ambition can be dangerous and is known to be destructive if not administered accordingly. It is a fine quality to have but can be catastrophic if abused. Ambition requires objective judgement, measured confidence, some level of risk and a decent sum of decency.

On black sheep, black markets, black magic, blackmails and black everything else, *bliksem,* here is what is truth; Black is the colour most prevalent in the absence of light. It is also the most heat absorbent of colours; colour being an illuminated part of a visibility spectrum in the presence of light. It is a little intriguing therefore that black is the resultant colour when there is no light, the only colour that is visible to the eye without illumination. The the only colour that thrives in the absence of light, black fills the void left by the absence of light. Figuratively, black represents importunity and strong will. This, bliksem, is what is truth on black everything.

42. Getting new names

This piece celebrates notable Africans, some of whom are probably well known internationally but most were unknown to the masses as at the time of writing this piece. The common feature of these people is that they have been positively influential to me personally. Each of the people written about in this piece has been influential to me in a major way. The piece is inspired by NoViolet Bulawayo's book, We Need New Names. We do need new names; names that redefine us; names that re-represent us and what we are about. From what I have seen, heard and read in different media, it seems we are getting new names.

Getting new names

We are not just many anymore, we are also one. We
are Goya, dead artists, dead sons, dead friends. We
came from little known villages, remained little
known, lived a little. Our lives are short. In the short
time that we lived, we were deep thinkers, tempters of
passion. We dared, we dreamed. In our brief life, we
tried, we inspired, we taught, we learnt. In our lives we
met the varied and played with the unique. In our
short lives we developed and got better. We introduced
the biggest change of all, we harboured the hope of
possibility. We walked the walk to freedom, we drew
and painted fellow freedom fighters. In our short lives,
we have been impactful. Though we left too early, we
left our mark. We are the arrested development,
legendary stories cut short, we came, we saw and
dearly departed before we could conquer.

We are B-B. We came from *Bluetown* to light blue
collars and black ties. Directing and managing G-N-I-
I-P, gross national income impacting productions.
They say we are leaders. We are the beginning of an
episode in the story of *Iemanja*. We are *corporate-
cats;* we sign big checks and look after big projects. We
are not fake and superficial, we have a unique story.
We have sad and happy stories; we represent the
lesson of perseverance. Named after herders, we stand
for steady guidance. We are recognizably fanatic and
inspired by higher powers. We are naturally humble,
which is why our confidence often stinks of arrogance.
The two, arrogance and humility are mutually inherent
in us. Those like us and those who know us better
know this. We are merchants of gems and yet we are
gems ourselves; one in many but one of many still.

We know that no one knows the future. This is what the weatherman said just another day the other day. We are Asa, the original beautiful imperfections. We sing songs, we sing of events, incidents and accidents. We lament and advise, celebrate and question out loud. We mourn our gone babies. To our little girls, we warn that they be careful if anybody say baby I love you. We hope that not just our voice is heard when we cry and die, pleading that we be left alone. For we know that our luck will not come if we wait for tomorrow while today wastes away. We have cried wolf about the fire at the mountain, but this time there is a fire. We advise that it is not this mountain that is worth climbing because all that is worth it is in us. As real as our frustration is about our *soldier-man* who fights another man's cause, it is the disappointment at our jailer that we grieve the most; an ignorant, a fellow prisoner, a confused fellow victim. We are angered, bruised and frustrated but we are loving too; this is probably something we picked from our beloved mums. To those gone, we wish peace; to those who are *yei*, we sing *wowowo*.

We are Omaru, we identify with old mythical spirits. We spread *procopian* ideas and thoughts of Con Fuseus, fellow false philosopher kings. We are bad scientists, we publish alternative knowledge; we data mine and mine data, we recognise patterns and devise expert algorithms and artificial intelligence with prudence. We are self-exiled, after green pastures and living foreign lives. We endure and adapt, we are early train riders, doctors of philosophy, star consultants and analysts of security. We thrive in opportunity; we create some where none existed. For luck we tarry not; we has to keep running. To rods and stuff we whisper, thou comfort me. While we are active, we endeavour to stride. While we live, we try and try. We represent the movement, we rejuvenate the philosophy; we compress the abstract, we stand for the stance and the way of the stance. We have beaten competition, we want nothing to do with best, we prefer better, we heard of perfection and that is whose trail we be after.

We are Jabba, we are cofounders of a genre. We gave style to local vocal identity; we kicked off a shit-storm of expression. Locally, we exist as Scar, national flag bearers. We are Mojo, we are the local political scientists. We are opinionated in this and that; we argue against the establishment, we orate a local sentiment on a social issue. We are Tuks, gifted, creative and foulmouthed *tshele* spinners. We speak of *konokono*, the essence; we tell it how we see it. If we have to, we can be hippie poets like *Lehipi la Mmoki*, we abuse uncommon vocabulary in vernacular. We can excel in a group and be a *Morafe*; we can mix and match languages like the United Nations assembly. For money, we work where we groove at. For a living, we stick to the rhythm while we speak to the music. And to music, we are the volume like Tumi. We sound smart, we are onto something. In our raps we speak of a revolution. Of this revolution we caution- *Fuck you take that shit outside.*

Our stories will be heard, our characters will resonate. Like Chima Adichie, we radiate the light from the torches of Chinua and Wole. We announce the *now-here* female revolution. Bred in the city of murder-*kwaBulawayo*, we are daughters of courageous women; our fathers span the spectrum of men categories. Our totems are animals, we are the mighty *Ndlovu* elephants, elaborate *Dube* zebras, we are a stampede of *Nyathi* buffaloe and flock together like the *Nyoni* birds. We are a herd of *Nkomo* cattle. We are descendants of Mzilikazi, dissenters and rebellious breakaways. We are not just here, we are from there and once conquered a small tribe here and another one there. Our history is rich, our stories are legendary and we will tell them. We will make the effort to preserve the mythical, the natural magic, the adventure, the pain of hell and the bliss of heaven that is our story. Understanding, conscious and aware of the duty it is to be who we are or who we choose to be; we will keep our cool, we will chin up, we will walk with heads held high. And if we find we need new names for new missions, NoViolet and such is who we will be.

We are Tembs Likle, the untypical inspiration, heroines in our own right. We are Pena, the first connectionists. We are Q in Queensland; quantum minded and ever advanced; *Afrostralian Nazarenes* and fathers of *Shlomo*. We are Zulu, we have friends in foreign lands. We are Tshepza, Thabza and Rita, we are the progress. We are Zee, last alphabetically and first academically. We are Zuza, KG and Fufa, nephews to great uncles. We are Mpumi, the *Afro deity*. We are Stoan and Zakes, loyal friends. We are Qondi, living miracles, evidences of hope. We are Crosby *Mwendalamphepo*, hardest of workers, best of companies.

We are Linda, primary school competitors and government economic planners. We are Tatts, quality individuals, ahead of our times. We are a key part of this story; we are Daila, co-creators of the new system. We are MaShiela and Bapaphi, knowledge increasers, national educators, talent scouts and foot soldiers of the revolution. We are Lempti, fellow believers in the seventh day, rest and relaxation. We are Best, we have represented the *dreadman* in the backyard of Ghandi and the African scholar in the institutions of Nobel laureates. We are Boomer, heads of families and new patriarchs. We are Solo, *nkhwinyas* and fellow exiles. And altogether, we are change, we are a rapid evolution, we are adapting, and the first thing we are doing is getting new names.

43. Abstract jabber

Eat, love and pray; mind, body and soul; junk in, junk out; no pain no gain; first in best dressed; These are some of life's simple lines on complex matters. This is what the *Abstract* is about, the simplified complexities. If one steadies and carefully seeks to understand, one will discover that the abstract is not a jabber at all. It is only referred to as jabber by those who do not attempt to understand it. The abstract has remained concealed and un-decoded for a long time because it was wrongly believed to be blather, a string of random unrelated phrases, it was inaccurately estimated to be not worth much to anybody. Sadly the delight of the abstract stayed hidden and was consequently accessible to the lucky, hardworking and ready few. The following is a true account of what is falsely known as the abstract jabber.

Abstract jabber

When time and condition afford an opportunity, thank powers that be. And then set about deciphering an abstract. Focus not on the abstracting text but the larger concept the words represent. The abstract will not have the typical footnote; there will be no translations and no fine-print. The abstract will not have a précis; the abstract is the précis. The abstract is for relevance, not logic. The abstract is a signature, its understanding is optional and its discernment is beneficial.

Even though the great conspiracy ignorantly proposes that the abstract is just a jabber, the truth is that the abstract is not a jabber. The conspiracy in this case has no speck of truth. The conspiracy is the exact opposite of the truth. The truth is, the abstract is a code, it represents something, abbreviates some concept, some creativity, some enterprise. Prominent speculators have alluded to all sorts of explanations and reputed conclusions on why the abstract is often mistaken for a jabber. The popular belief is that it is an abstract ramble, not worth much to anyone. Because of the sustained conspiracy against its true intent, the abstract remained concealed and un-decoded for a long time; it was ignored by conventional thinking and shunned by technical scholars.

The abstract was written such that the rules of logic which are usually vital in most concepts do not apply to the texts of the abstract. It is therefore unsurprising that conventionalism ignored the abstract and categorised it as empty chatter. A blind pursuit of logic is why conventionalism failed to reveal and decode the *abstract* and why it was easier to classify it as jabber. Having tried all they could, conventionalists finally realised that no artillery of logic could *bruteforce* the code of the encrypted abstract. Rather than seek alternative ways to decode it, they resorted to dismissing the abstract.

For a long time, multiple attempts to decipher the abstract have proved futile. *Resultantly,* the gist of the abstract remained hidden, unknown stayed the enterprise represented by the abbreviation. Sadly too, exclusivity became the delight of this enterprise. As with most other phenomena, rumour became the bitch of abstract. Some rumour claims that the abstract is about users and the gloom of abusers. In other circles, rumour has it that the abstract is about the secret; and some other rumour claims the abstract comprises the golden rule. Whereas in other corners, there are rumours of *Longevitists* as subscripts and keepers of the abstract. In other crevices, rumour claims that the here-and-now and the heat of the moment is what the abstract is about. And so forth and so on the theories go. For a long time the meaning and benefit of abstract remained accessible to a handful of *anglecovers*, the lucky, hardworking and ready few prepared to pay a little more thought to the abstract.

According to another theory on the abstract, it takes strength to profess and it takes profession to actualize. How then do the weak gain power? Weakness is not the absence of strength, but the absence of power. To gain power, the weak must use their strength. Using this strength, they must profess. The atomic disparity between the mighty and the humble is that the former use their strength to profess. As the theory goes, this is the attitude most absent in the mentality of the weak. As relative as weakness is, a respective opposite of a particular weakness will obstinately be superior. This is the power of profession inherent in the respective opposite of any measure of weakness. The strength to profess exists naturally in all living-things and rarely runs out. In its smallest of measures, this strength will always be sufficient to qualify and differentiate strength over weakness. This strength is superior and is the better alternative to self-preservation relative to any weakness. In a similar context, *nothing* has nothing to do with anything worth something; it takes something to make anything, it take something to be anything.

Another hearsay on the abstract speculates that when one door of misery closes, another, of opportunity opens. Some versions of this speculation claim that when one door of opportunity closes, another door of misery opens. The latter version advises disciples of this philosophy to be ever ready for the unexpected. This is dismissed as pessimistic by critics of the same philosophy who counsel that it is impossible to prepare for unexpected events because they are unpredictable and impossible to anticipate. Critics of the pessimist add that if it is not expected, it cannot be pre-empted. But it can, according to the *philosophy of readiness*. It starts with expectation; the unexpected has to be expected. When it is expected, it can be prepared for and possibly altered if it unravels. But how is the unexpected expected? What exactly gets expected in this case and what validates this expectation? Apparently there is a way; *Abstractionists* have summarised it as being *ready for whatever*. The *readiness* and its object are abstract, relative and personal.

Frustrated and with little understanding, the conventionalists turned the verses of the abstract into song; work conquers all, never too late, better late than never. With no *deeperstanding*, they sing; now is the time, do it now, just do it. Little do they realise that although it may be abstract, this is no jabber.

44. Nuff is Enuff

To every pursuit comes a time of completion. Abstraxion is only a phase of a greater event, a perspective of a bigger picture. Just as Amen marks the end of a prayer, *Nuff is Enuff* marks the end of an undertaking, the culmination of a pursuit. In any sustained pursuit, there is a point where enough is enough. Whatever this pursuit is, whatever it is for, whatever significance it may embody; enough is enough at some point. *Nuff is Enuff* is that point for Abstraxion.

Nuff is Enuff

What is it all for? It must have significance. It cannot just be for personal vanity, it must be bigger than that.

This is what is it for. It serves to highlight the small time and glorify effort, though effort alone is rarely enough and has come short most days on its own. So it is not effort on its own glorified in the said significance, it is effort and more. And the small times, they cannot just be highlighted. They must be activated, breathed and chipped at. Like waves, they must be surfed for however long they last. When the small times are highlighted and effort glorified, something else lurks in the ulterior. This is the demonstration of commitment to the significance. The significance is what it is for, why the small time matters. In my case, it is expression of thought, transmission of perspective, dispersal of insight. It is for whomever it concerns and to whomever wills. It should not take any more than concern and will to get started, it may require more from the concerned and willing as soon as they are concerned, and willing to take in the insight. It starts simply and gets abstracted in the process. At its most abstract, it is about better, bigger and greater, over and over until it is done, and only then is it enough.

To each, only a certain amount can be given. Those who attempt to find the limit of this certain amount ultimately realise it is a wild goose chase. The discerning few realise that at some point, it must be enough and no more is necessary. These few realise there exists this point where one cannot take anymore, a point where one cannot give anymore. There are times when one does not have any to give. There are times also, when one does not want to give. The latter situation is advised against although the best gifts are rarely purely voluntary and usually subtly selfish. There are times when possession is of higher priority than sentiment. Such is the case with the flow of credit in the commercial world. A given amount of cash earned from a reluctant debtor has the same buy-power as the same amount given by a supposedly willing party. It is good to give, especially when the gift makes a difference to the *givee*. The giving is even better to the giver when it serves some subtly selfish need, reason or ambition. So on the possibility of endless giving and taking, one is inclined to endorse the possibility but one knows it is a remote possibility. Nature is such that very few systems are infinite. Many systems have a termination point, a point of expiration. This is the point when enough is enough and the system cannot operate any more.

The idea is that when it all comes to an end, which it ultimately does because nothing lasts forever; that by then the message is true to some, relevant to some and inspiring to some. The idea is that in the end proverbs get created of this phenomenon; that poems get fashioned to rhyme the same concept. When enough is enough and it is done for the time being; it should appeal not superficially, impress not fleetingly and should certainly not accompany only briefly. It must be the firmament of permanence, it will be finer than average in every quality measure. Superior will be the relative attribute of every effort committed to it. Even then, effort will not be its exclusive virtue because this personal pursuit is multi virtuous. If it is established that personal pursuits are in vain, then any such pursuit must not demonstrate nor acknowledge vanity in any way. Every piece of work is valuable; the worker need not be ignorant of the value of their work. In the end; one must be proud of it all, their personal pursuits. If it is worth pursuing personally then it usually is a labour of love, pursuit of an ideal and ultimately, a life well lived.

Enough is enough, everything in moderation. Just as excessive philosophy dominates common sense; as disproportionate power turns men evil and as excess wealth corrupts charity, enough is enough. Whatever it is for, whatever significance it may represent, enough is enough.

45. !Forfarksake

The language in this piece may seem provocative to the sensitive reader but the message will make sense to the open minded reader. The bottom line is, none of it was just for the heck of it, none of it was for *farksake*.

!Forfarksake

When you have to, you gotta cut a *bitch*, right?

Strict thinker, strict talker; excuse the title; it is time I said my piece. And while I'm at it, might as well run a few past you, let me utter a few to you *infukinfact*. I think you are uptight, too uptight; strict about everything, worried about everything, negative about everything, mad at everything. I think you are prisoner to your narrowness and negativity and I think you could do with a *spliff*. That's it, I think you could use a really good screw. Go for a jog if screwing isn't for you, take a walk if you are too heavy for a run, just do something, sitting still makes you stink. And just so you know, this isn't for farksake, this is to build you. If you can't live with that, I don't give a ... Yea, you do the math.

The other day, one deliberated and summarised personal *Leverage*. The semantics of the story of Leverage are slightly obscure, the theme may not be obvious to some either. The theme is that Leverage or not, dog must get bone. So if this has not materialised somehow in the piece of Leverage, let it be known here and now. Let it be known that the way one sees it, this *Leverage*, it has to be calculated. The ways of advancing the cause of one's purpose have to be leveraged against all other ways detrimental to this cause. If others feel that one's cause is irrelevant to theirs, they must be concerned. They must be concerned because it is their irrelevance at odds with a force of nature. And if they can't let one be then they best bring it on, because for his cause, one will stand up to anything and anybody. Anyone must stand up to anything or anybody that threatens their purpose.

False prophet, there is no denying the power of nature, the natural disasters, the elements that turn destructive on certain occasions. There is no feigning agnostic tendencies to natural magic, luck and the damned accidents. So if there is a power out there, some sun god, then it is possible that they can hear one. And if they can hear one then they can hear all; which means each of us can intercede on our own behalves and pray for our *effing* selves. And if the supreme can respond to one, then why not to the other also? If the supreme can nod to one then must surely nod to another. I trust your getting the words; I hope your understanding them. I ask that you stop claiming to communicate to the gods on my behalf and let me pray for myself. And let me find my god too. I am onto you, false prophet. I hope your indulgent but non-creative ass gets found one of these days. I find it disgusting that those closest to you know your phony tendencies. I think it is repulsive that they know that you're fake and have found some cheap trade to exploit. And your not even good at it. Much as I would like to say farkyu, I just won't; rather I hope that you awaken to yourself. How can yours be a noble cause when you create an additional barrier to what is meant to be and must be a direct connection to the sacred energies. Either way, I know you will have to answer to yourself someday. In the meantime, enjoy it while it lasts bitch.

Doubter, you think it's uninspired? Don't kid yourself. It never goes down if it isn't. It always has to be and always is. This has been the case for every piece of the Abstraxion. All including this here piece had a fair dose of inspiration. The suggestion that any part of the Abstraxion is uninspired must be rejected outright. It mustn't be accepted that some perspective of the way one sees things is somewhat insufficient. Suggestions like these are malicious and propagandist. The way anyone sees is enthused, especially when it isn't for *farksake*. Freedom, they say is when you do what pleases you at your convenience. This here, is my freedom, it is wherever, whenever, about whatever, seen, heard, imagined, taught, thought and felt. If you don't feel it, think whatever of it doubter but don't think it uninspired. It farkin wasn't, it was not for *farksake* either.

Epilogue

To you reader;

The best and last part of Abstraxion is reserved for you, the reader. Assuming you have read all the pieces of Abstraxion, I will not attempt to explain the subtle context of the abstracts. My attempt may not make much of a difference to your existing understanding. If anything, my explanation may spoil your perfect, personal comprehension of Abstraxion.

Why abstracts? A friend whom I asked to pre-read some of the earlier pieces once asked me this question. Abstracts seemed to me the best way to present the varying, multiple events, topics, histories, subjects and themes that I cover in the different pieces. Over time, abstracts became all I know. The knowledge I have on any subject is only a small subset of all there is on the given matter. The abstracts represent this aspect and also acknowledge the existence of various other perspectives on the same subject. My abstracts summarise a thought on one or two of several perspectives to any idea. The pieces propose that nothing is absolute; that anything can be perceived differently from different angles.

The pieces of Abstraxion were penned over 4 years, usually only when I had a spare hour or two from the occupations of the day. I started writing the pieces when I was studying for my PhD. Writing the pieces was a break from academic writing and post graduate research, which have their rules. The pieces became a way to freely express the ambiguities clouding my view at the time. I enjoyed writing each piece, I liked that I paid very little regard to grammar and syntax. I also wanted each piece to be independently meaningful because I initially had no intentions of compiling the pieces into a book. So at the time of writing, each piece had to be relevant on its own, each abstract was meant to be a unique masterpiece. It was not until I had more than half of the 50 or so pieces that I thought it would be good to stack them into a book. So in my endeavour to decipher the scientific, philosophical, historic, technical, legendary, spiritual and mathematical, I found that conventional rules of grammar and logic were sometimes an obstacle to my unravelling masterpiece. So excuse the occasional disregard for the conventions of grammar; its my art.

The pieces of Abstraxion are about creativity, opportunity, gratefulness, eloquence, readiness, objectivity, critique and peculiarity; to list a few. I have come to believe that each of us is peculiar; If you look inside of yourself and find that you are not peculiar, you are not looking hard enough. Peculiarity is personal and right within each of us.

The message of Abstraxion is what you make of it. I wrote it such that whatever you get from a particular piece or from the book as a whole is worth your while. I hope you read it with an open mind and have made something out of it. I hope you have learnt something, smiled at some dodgy line, wondered at yet another illogical proposition or acknowledged some fact. Although the pieces are not a series of events describing some story, they are individually complete and collectively paint a picture. What this picture is and what it means to you is your privilege as the reader.

I am proud of this book and could write another book about it. But even as I write the epilogue, I know its impact will be realised once it gets perused by the reader. So I thank you for taking the time to read my work. Thank you for attempting to understand it and for getting it; I know you get it. If you don't, thank you for admitting it and please read it again. When you have read it again and this time you get it, thanks again. – Oarabile Maruatona.

Glossary

Contextual definitions for some of the uncommon words and phrases used throughout the book.

Abstractionists: A painter, singer, writer and thinker of Abstract.
Abstraxion: The art, philosophy and science of abstraction.
Adhoc: Technically decentralised and independent of existing support infrastructure.
Afro deity: African deity.
Afrostralian: African Australian.
Alphabitat: Habitat of the Alpharean.
Alpharean: The human of the future. Also known as the Homo-alpha.
Alphareans: Humans of the 40s centuries.
Ambitionist: Chaser of ambition.
Amphibius: Amphibian species.
Amy: Amy Winehouse.
Anglecovers: Conscious and committed to living purposefully. Covering as many life angles as one can in their everyday activities.
Anti-tide: Against the norm.
Any is any: Nothing is absolute. Anything can happen.
Arite: Alright.
Atlantica: Old century continent.
Badimo: Gods.
Basicness: Foundational.
Bee busyness: As busy as a bee.
Biblus: Bible.
Bitch: Coward.
Bliksem: Exclamation.
Bloody awesome: Bloody awesome.
Bluetown: A suburb of Francistown, Botswana, Africa.

240

Botho: Ubuntu. An ideology of community and kinsmanship.
Bruteforce: To breach a technical defence by several trials.
Budgies: Budgie smuggler
Bustardry: Ill-mannered and disrespectful.
Calligraph: Represent graphically.
Carpe momentum: Seize the moment.
Catting and mousing: Running in circles.
Charactery-stick: Quality of character.
Chardi kala: All shall be well. Sikh ideology.
Chemicalised: Substantially complemented with chemical additives.
Chuana: Tswana. African tribe.
Conal: Third.
Confuseunist: Sympathetic to the ideas of Con Fuseus.
Congans: The people of the first Congo.
Con-modity: commodity
Con-munity: Community of the Con-Pression treatise sympathisers.
Con-niving: conniving
Consumerist: Chiefly interested in consuming.
Contura: Century.
Convalian: Legendary army of the first Congo.
Con-victions: conviction
Corporate cats: Working in the corporate sector.
Crude will: Strong willpower.
Crunk: Too drunk.
Cryptiques: Cryptic abstractions. Deeply abstracted facts.
Cum laude: With distinction.
Deeperstanding: Deep understanding.
Destination worthwhile: Worthwhile destination.
Dis-appearance: Disappearance.
Doeth: Does.
Doodle scribble: Written gibberish.

Dreadman: Anyone that identifies with the Rastafarian philosophy of love and peace.
Dube: Zebra. Also a prominent lastname in the Ndebele tribe.
Effing: F-ing.
Ella: Ella Fitzgerald
Eppur si mouve: And yet it moves.
Essentiality: Being essential.
Everydays: everyday events
Excusating: In the habit of giving excuses for own faults.
Excusez la sous estimation: Excuse my over estimation of your intelligence.
Expressor: Conveyor of ideas.
Ex-sential: Expressly essential
Farksake: No noble sake. No good reason.
Faux-truth: False truth. Seemingly true but false.
Femto technology: Future future generation technology.
Flash-forward: Imagination of the future.
Fock-all: Nothing.
Foetally invasive: With technical capacity to scan a foetus in a womb.
Givee: The given. The recipient of a gift.
Greeding: Greedily craving.
Habitualised: Turned into habit.
Have nots: The poor.
Hisself: Himself.
Homosonic: Sounding the same.
How-unfortunately-ever: Sadly however.
Iemanja: African water goddess. A mother figure.
Ill: Elaborate
Imaginatory-capacity: Breadth of imagination and depth of perception.
Infukinfact: In fact
Inhidvo: In High Definition

Insectus: Insect.
Intercedory: On behalf of the bemused.
Invested at interest: An interest accruing financial investment.
Invitro: In a test tube.
Journeywoman: The travelling woman.
Kalanga: African tribe.
Kgarari: Kalahari desert.
Khukhi: Khukhi.
Khulu: A man on his death bed. (Credit Motlapele Morule)
Konokono: The essence. The core.
Konsapien: An old dynasty of the rulers of the first Congo.
Krafuta: Graphite.
KwaBulawayo: A place of murder. The second largest Zimbabwean city of Bulawayo.
Landlordship: The Croesus. Extremely wealthy.
Lehipi la mmoki: Hippie poet
Lestrania: A country.
Lestranian: Resident of Lestrania.
Lifachi: Land.
Lifefull: Lasting a lifetime.
Lifelike: Seeming like life.
Longevitist: Subscript of Longevity. Sympathetic to the ideology of the long term.
Mannlich: Male.
Mattahu perfection: Perfection as presented by Apostle Matthew.
Mea culpa mundo: Forgive me world.
Meine Likle: My Likle. My lover.
Mich nicht: Not me.
Modernly: Broadcast in recent technology.
Modimo Nkutswa: God steal me.
Morafe: Tribe.
Mundo Historius: History of the world.

Mwendalamphepo: Easily shaken by wind. A wanderer.

Nano technology: Future generation technology.

Naturel: A natural reactivity.

Nazarenes: Sympathetic to the biblical Nazareth and its significance as the home of Jesus Christ.

Ndlovu: Elephant. Also a prominent lastname in the Ndebele tribe.

Neglect laziness: Laziness justified by some excuse.

Neosapien: The new man

Nkhwinya: Mate. Friend.

Nkomo: Cow. Also a prominent lastname in the Ndebele tribe.

Nowheria: A country.

Nows: Present moments.

Nyathi: Buffalo. Also a prominent lastname in the Ndebele tribe.

Nyoni: Bird. Also a prominent lastname in the Ndebele tribe.

Overstood: Deep understanding.

Peculiarly: Arranged in a peculiar manner.

Penners: Recorders of the revolution.

Pen-paper-pursuit: Writing as a career.

Personalism: Personal in design.

Philosophication: Corruption by philosophy.

Precurses: Comes or occurs before.

Pre-poverty-levels: Before poverty could be measured.

Pressury: Emotionally pressing.

Procopian: Relating to the writings of Procopius of Caesarea

Promptu: A sudden urge to act or move.

Push meets shove: Critical time.

Qaeda: Home. Base.

Que sera: Que sera sera. Whatever will be, will be.

Rebeligious: Rebellious and religious.

Recollector: Story teller.

Reflectory: In contemplation.
Reptilus: Reptile.
Restedness: Relaxed and refreshed.
Resultantly: As a result.
Revolvement: A 360 degree physical revolution.
Ritualities: Ceremonial rituals.
Sa'hra: Sahara desert.
Sabach: A day of rest.
Salarium: Profits from the salt trade.
Saltarean: A period when salt was the best-selling commodity in global trade.
Saltology: Study of the chemistry, history and trade of salt.
Sayeth: Says.
Sebakanyana se: This little chance.
Seeth: Sees.
Selflessly selfish: Selfish for a communal cause.
Self-preservationist: Committed to the preservation of self.
Self-tribulise: Pay tribute to self. Write own history.
Setho: About Botho.
Shango: World.
Sheba-da: Watch out.
Shebeen-queen: Female owner and operator of a small, homebrewing enterprise.
Shlomo: Solomon
Shuka: Shuka.
Sick: Sophisticated
Societally significant: Holding a high position in society.
Sociologicals: Social and logical.
Some-a-times: Sometimes.
Spects: Spectacles.
Spliff: A drag or two of smoke. Symbolism for internal cleansing and uplifting.
Spotable: Easily spotted.

Squeezy: Economically pressing.
State zeta: Self defined state of completion.
Strive and thrive: Livelihood
Susu ilela suswane: Tswana proverb. The older of two deaf individuals must only earn respect by respecting the younger.
Syntho: Synthetic.
Taxiderms: Stuffed replicas.
Technoholic: Almost totally dependent on technology.
Templative: Template by design.
Theorium passos: Theory of passion
Thor: Norse god of thunder, lightning and strength.
Thoth: Ancient Egyptian god of magic, writing and science.
Tings: Things
Torgos: Vulture.
Travellingman: The journeyman.
Trueself: True self.
Tshele: Propaganda and fact spun and mixed.
Tswana: African tribe.
Unconceal: Reveal.
Un-phenomenal: Not remarkable.
Unstillness: Impactful movement. Work.
Upping Ante: Upping the ante for impact.
Visualisor-contextualisor: Visualising and contextualising impactful ideas.
Vocanomics: Vocabulary economics. Efficiency with words.
Wall streets: Investment, financial brokerage and exchange institutions.
Wathauring: Indigenous Australian tribe.
Whitney: Whitney Houston.
Wishfulness: Empty hope.
Wordly-economic: Resourceful with words.
Wowowo: Unknown. (Credit Bukola Elemide)
Wurrundjeri: Indigenous Australian tribe.

Yei: Unknown. (Credit Bukola Elemide)
YHWH-SOS: God save our souls.
Yown: Your own. Yours.
Zeroness: State of mental pause.

Formal names (Getting new names)

Below are the formal names of some of the characters described in *Getting new names*. Some of these individuals have been my good friends, others I have not met yet but they all inspire me and are great role models.

Asa: Bukola Elemide

Bapaphi: Lovemore Ntogwa

B-B: Balisi Bonyongo

Best: Olerato Duna

Boomer: Buyani Muncele Shabani

Chima Adichie: Chimamanda Ngozi Adichie

Chinua: Chinua Achebe

Crosby: Dick Chisenga

Daila: David Moroka

Goya: Mompoloki Oneilwe

Jabba: Jabulani Tsambo

Lehipi La Mmoki: Keabetswe Modimoeng

Lempti: Keaboka Gaelaiwe

Linda: Goitsemodimo Mathodi

MaShiela: Ruth Mazhani

Mojo: Motlapele Morule

Morafe: Kgaugelo Choabi, Khulane Morule, Lerothodi Moagi

Mpumi: NoMpumelelo

NoViolet Bulawayo: Zandile Tshele

Pena: Oabona Dadani

Q: Mpho Utlwang

Qondi: Qondile Khumalo

Rita: Masego Maika

Scar: Thato Matlhabaphiri

Solo: Ntjidzi Kombani

Stoan: Mooketsi Maruatona

Tatts: Thatayaone Mpuchane

Tembs Likle: Thembi Dube Omaru

Thabza: Thabo Khumoetsile

Tshepza: Tshepiso Mokhuni

Tuks: Tumelo Kepadisa

Tumi: Boitumelo Molekane

Wole: Wole Soyinka

Zakes: Ezekiel Keoreng

Zee: Zwikamu Dubani

Zulu: Siamisang Rangwanamong

Abstraxion| Oarabile Maruatona

Made in the USA
Middletown, DE
05 February 2018